"Anticipation and pleasure encapsulate the essence of seed swapping for me. Sowing new acquisitions obtained from fellow enthusiasts who had a glint in their eye of the beauty or the food that they were sharing. Hopefully, the next generation of pleasure-seeking seed swappers is well on its way and this lovely book will keep them on the path of discovery."

Andy Jackson
HEAD OF WAKEHURST PLACE, ROYAL BOTANIC GARDENS, KEW, ENGLAND

"The Soil Association recognizes the importance of conserving, not only the genetic diversity of our food supply, but also the skills and knowledge of saving seed in growers both professional and amateur. We have already lost thousands of varieties due to the concentration of seed production in a relatively small number of companies and this trend is set to continue. Home saving and swapping of seed is one way to fight against this and retain some sovereignty and ownership of what we grow and eat."

Ben Raskin
HEAD OF HORTICULTURE, SOIL ASSOCIATION, UK

"There is little doubt that this book will be a 'must have' reference at Seedy Sunday. It will fit into a large pocket or bag. It is not only a delight to hold and beautiful to browse through, but a source of valuable information for use on a coffee table, as a reference source at any Seedy Sunday, or for me to keep in my community garden shed."

Alan Phillips
CHAIRPERSON, SEEDY SUNDAY, BRIGHTON, ENGLAND

"There is nothing more important in our times than saving seeds and swapping seeds. We are faced with a seed emergency caused by rapid disappearance of seed diversity, the replacement of renewable seeds with nonrenewable, patented seeds, and the perverse idea that seed saving and seed sharing is an 'intellectual property crime.' *Seedswap* will help spread the seeds of freedom."

Dr. Vandana Shiva
SEED ACTIVIST AND FOUNDER OF NAVDANYA INTERNATIONAL

"Seeds are the source of life and this book will help you to reach that source."

Satish Kumar
EDITOR-IN-CHIEF, RESURGENCE AND ECOLOGIST

"The amount of interest in seed swaps is growing all the time and it's great to see a book that not only tells you about the 'why do' but also the 'how to' of seed swapping and the practical art of saving seeds as well."

Neil Munro
MANAGER, THE HERITAGE SEED LIBRARY

Josie Jeffery

Seedswap

The gardener's guide

to saving and swapping seeds

ROOST
BOOKS

Boston 2013

Roost Books

An imprint of Shambhala Publications, Inc.
Horticultural Hall
300 Massachusetts Avenue
Boston, Massachusetts 02115
roostbooks.com

First published in the UK in 2012 by Leaping Hare Press
210 High Street
Lewes
East Sussex BN7 2NS
United Kingdom
www.leapingharepress.co.uk

This book was conceived, designed, and produced by
Leaping Hare Press

CREATIVE DIRECTOR Peter Bridgewater
PUBLISHER Susan Kelly
COMMISSIONING EDITOR Monica Perdoni
SENIOR DESIGNER James Lawrence
SENIOR EDITOR Jayne Ansell
DESIGNER Clare Barber
PROJECT EDITOR Susie Behar
ILLUSTRATORS Joanna Kerr, Julie Payne
COVER ILLUSTRATOR Melvyn Evans

Printed in China
Color origination by Ivy Press Reprographics
9 8 7 6 5 4 3 2 1
First Edition

Distributed in the United States by Random House, Inc.,
and in Canada by Random House of Canada Ltd

Library of Congress Cataloging-in-Publication Data
Jeffery, Josie.
Seedswap: the gardener's guide to saving and
swapping seeds / Josie Jeffery.
p.   cm
Includes index.
ISBN 978-1-61180-091-3 (hardcover: alk. paper)
1. Seeds—Harvesting. 2. Seeds—Collection and
preservation. 3. Seed exchanges. I. Title.
SB118.3.J44 2013
631.5'21—dc23
2013004016

Contents

Foreword

It's easy to forget the extraordinary wonders of nature. The story of Jack and the Beanstalk is an entertaining fairy tale that one generation of parents after another read to their children. The cycle of nature is repeated and renewed with relish, because the plant never fails to inspire awe in little children. How can such a small bean grow so tall that it reaches out to the heavens?

As a gardener and seed saver, I take it for granted that a small tomato seed, less than ⅛ inch (3 mm) in diameter, can grow within months to a plant 3 feet (1 m) high and wide, with scores of deliciously warm, sun-blessed tomatoes, such as "Gardener's Delight" or "Brandywine," that are just waiting to be eaten.

Many adults, even gardeners, consider seed sowing, let alone seed saving and storing, to be black arts, and they stand in awe of those who have these skills. Now *Seedswap* shares all, bursting the bubble of those myths, and showing how all careful gardeners can and should save and sow their own seeds. Seed saving, storing, and sowing all require some care and nurturing to make sure that plants remain true and strong. One of the great strengths of this book is that it covers all three aspects, while almost half of it showcases a wide variety of plants from which seed can be saved.

Seed saving and sowing are a crucial part of a much wider sustainability and self-reliance agenda, where "small is beautiful" and where we must think globally and act locally. Ever since humankind evolved from being hunter-gatherers to farmers, communities have had a vested interest in making sure the quality and security of food supplies. This included the saving, storing, and sowing of the most reliable and productive varieties of crops.

Multinational companies that often export and import food across continents have also recognized the importance of seed varieties that not only produce crops that can be transported easily, but also have a long shelf life in stores and look good any time of the year. These companies often create a monopoly on certain seeds (F1 hybrid varieties, for example), which have to be bought from them; it becomes uneconomic for them to sell a wide variety of seeds, especially ones that have adapted over generations to a local environment.

Seed saving and swapping can be fun, too. The Seedy Sunday event in Brighton, England, started just over a decade ago on the first Sunday in February. Now thousands of people come out of their winter hibernation for this community event, to swap seeds, meet old friends, buy seed potatoes, obtain heritage varieties, have coffee and cake, and listen to talks. See www.seedysunday.org.

There is little doubt that this book will be a "must have" reference at Seedy Sunday. It is not only a delight to hold and beautiful to browse through, but a source of valuable information for use on a coffee table, a reference source at any Seedy Sunday, or for me to keep in my community garden shed.

Alan Phillips
CHAIRPERSON, SEEDY SUNDAY, BRIGHTON, ENGLAND

Introduction

My earliest "swaps," in the formative arena of the school playground, were about dinosaurs, the space race, or my football heroes. Our motivations were to get the whole set or the rarest card—in my case, the space shuttle! Seeds are somewhat like the space shuttle—a capsule preserving life through space and time, often in hostile conditions, but with all the essential requirements for survival onboard.

Seed swapping did not enter my head until I started to train as a gardener at the Royal Botanic Gardens, Kew, England. Since its inception in 1759, Kew has acquired, shared, and swapped seeds with growers and scientists. In the early years, during the "age of discovery," wonders and marvels arrived from all over the known world. Over the next 200 years, Kew helped to move seeds across the globe to produce new crops for food, drinks, fiber, and medicines. We shared these seeds through a list known as the *Index Seminum*.

The conservation potential of seeds was recognized in the 1970s, with the creation of a new scientific research program at Wakehurst Place. It began in a small chapel and consisted of one researcher, a technician, and a young doctoral research student. Forty years on, it has grown to be one of the world's largest plant conservation projects, with 11 percent of the world's plants stored in the freezing vaults of Kew's Millennium Seed Bank. The project has also funded new seed banks, which now form a global network striving to conserve 25 percent of the world's seed-bearing plants by 2020.

Storage is only one part of the conservation journey. Our ambition is to use these plants to offer innovative solutions to the challenges faced in providing us all with enough food, shelter, clothing, medicines, and fresh water. To do this, our seeds have to remain alive and usable, and we have to be ready to help out anyone in need.

My own research on one of Britain's rarest trees, the Plymouth pear (*Pyrus cordata*), has shown that it can be used in breeding programs with common varieties of pear and could be used to increase disease resistance and drought tolerance. Wild relatives of crop plants often have a range of attributes that plant breeders can use to increase potential production. Increasing salt tolerance in grain crops is a real challenge for the future in some of the world's "bread baskets." Wild plants may well provide the enhanced tolerance needed. Kew's Millennium Seed Bank is a fundamental part of a global partnership that aims to collect and conserve the relatives of our vital crop plants to enable such crucial research to take place. For interested readers, we've just published an account of the history of the Millennium Seed Bank in *The Last Great Plant Hunt, The Story of Kew's Millennium Seed Bank*, that explains the science in lay terms.

Having experienced central Africa in the middle of a great drought and seen at first hand the reliance of people, livestock, and wildlife on wild plants, I am absolutely convinced that conserving seeds is vital for our future. The act of conserving seeds has the potential to create local food security, and when conditions are right for sowing, seeds can be shared and can help enable communities to survive drought.

It is perhaps too much to dream that children may one day swap seeds in the playground. Although they are not as scary as a *T. rex* or as engaging

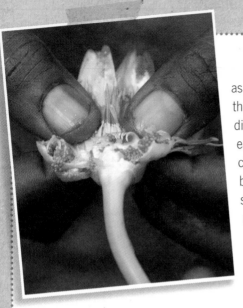

as Pokémon, Hello Kitty, or the latest craze, the key for us has been to engender a sense of discovery and adventure that was prevalent in earlier times. "The Great Plant Hunt" treasure chests, each containing a miniature seed bank, have been sent by Kew to every state-funded primary school (the same as an elementary school) in Britain (about 22,000 schools). Children can hunt for, discover, identify, dry, store, and swap their own seeds. It has proven so successful that the "Hunt Goes On"!

Anticipation and pleasure encapsulate the essence of seed swapping for me. Sowing new acquisitions obtained from fellow enthusiasts who had a glint in their eye of the beauty or the food that they were sharing. Hopefully, the next generation of pleasure-seeking seed swappers is well on its way and this wonderful book will keep them on the path of discovery.

Andy Jackson

HEAD OF WAKEHURST PLACE,
ROYAL BOTANIC GARDENS, KEW

SEED SWAPPING

WHAT IS SEED SWAPPING?

Seed swapping is about engaging with your community, sharing seeds with friends, neighbors, and relatives, and exchanging knowledge and ideas. At the same time, this fascinating activity makes it more probable that the genetic integrity of a plant is preserved and passed on.

This book covers the what, who, how, and why of seed swapping and seed saving. It advises where to start and how to get involved with the worldwide horticultural campaign to "save our seeds." The work of seed-activist individuals and groups is highlighted with inspirational tips and tales, and there is insight into the practices of major seed companies and how this has affected seed diversity and how "seed breeding" affects the future of plants. The work of seed collections and seed banks is explored, and advice is given on how to collect, clean, store, preserve, and raise seeds. The second part of the book contains an extensive plant directory, which is full of advice on how to grow plants from "seed to seed."

I have enjoyed seed saving for all of my gardening career. For me, it is one of the most exciting of garden tasks, and it represents the end of the season, a time for reflection. I enjoy the whole seed-saving process and sharing my garden's seed bounty with my friends and the community.

ABOVE Collecting seeds from my garden—not only a lot of fun but meaningful, too.

"Saving seed is a duty to the earth and to future generations."

DR. VANDANA SHIVA, FOUNDER OF NAVDANYA

WHY SWAP SEEDS?

Seed swapping is a means of exchanging surplus seeds as a goodwill gesture and usually takes place at organized gatherings for novice and seasoned gardeners. Participants trade their seeds and knowledge in a local community center or someone's house, or even via a "round robin" sweed swap.

With increases in the cost of living, seed swapping is a great way of becoming more self-sufficient in the ornamental garden as well as the fruit and vegetable garden. Saving and swapping seeds have a wealth of benefits, from the financial advantage to maintaining food security and protecting biodiversity, rare species, and seed genetics. It also helps to disseminate the practices and ideas of other cultures, that may be linked to particular plant species and their varieties. Seeds have the ability to travel great distances, and those with the greatest cultural significance tend to get transported by people as they move around the globe.

Swapping seeds expands the plant variety in a "swapper's" garden. At seed swaps, a wealth of local knowledge and wisdom can be exchanged, about what works—or doesn't work—in your microclimate, and you will probably discover new and exciting plants. Keeping things "local" helps the community become independent from seed manufacturers who tend to have control over the availability and variety of seeds.

Although seed saving has a long history, global events, such as Seedy Saturday and Seedy Sunday, only began in 1990. They enable communities to come together to share seeds and gardening stories. Seasoned seed-swap gardeners incorporate collecting seeds into their gardening routine specifically for seed-swapping events, and the ever-increasing popularity of these occasions has gained the interest of eager novices, too.

ABOVE AND BELOW Seed-swap events are increasingly popular internationally and provide a great opportunity for enthusiasts to source new seeds and mix with like-minded people.

"Seeds are, in a sense, suitcases in which people can transport their cultures with them . . . Many families have brought their favorite seeds on tremendous journeys."

MIKE SZUBERLA, ORGANIZER OF A SEED SWAP IN TOLEDO, OHIO

GETTING INVOLVED

Today, seed-swapping events happen all around the world, and if you are interested, it isn't hard to find one, whether it be at your local community center, community garden, or online.

ATTENDING A SEED SWAP

The Internet has masses of information on seed-swapping events. It is worth asking at any local community gardens, too. It is better to ask around in your area, because it is more probable that you'll find plants that will grow well in the conditions provided by your local climate.

START A "ROUND ROBIN" SEED SWAP

Swap seeds without having to pay for the rent of a venue by starting a seed-swapping chain.

- **Collect names** of the willing participants and provide the final list of names to everyone involved.
- **Send a package** filled with your surplus seeds to the next person on the list.
- **The next person** will then take one packet of seeds from the package and replace it with some more seeds.
- **The package is sent** to the next person on the list, who removes and replaces as above.
- **The chain carries on** until the last person on the list mails the package (which should now contain a completely different combination of seeds) back to the original organizer.

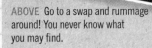

ABOVE Go to a swap and rummage around! You never know what you may find.

SALAD BURNETT

LEFT Write any useful information about the seeds on the front of the envelope.

SEED CIRCLES

A seed circle is a group of friends or community garden buddies who each sign up to save seeds from one or two kinds of plant. At the end of the growing season, each person saves seeds and arranges to share or exchange surplus with the rest of the circle.

Organizing a seed circle is really easy. This is what you need to get started:

- **An organizer**—you!
- **A dedicated group**—it can be small or large.
- **A sign-up form**—to collect everyone's contact details.
- **An information sheet**—to include important tips, such as how to save and store seeds, and your contact details.
- **A spare moment**—to check in on everyone's progress.
- **Good-quality, fresh, nonhybrid seeds**—to start your circle.

ABOVE Check your seeds thoroughly before a swap to make sure they are fresh and healthy.

BELOW Seal your seeds in small labeled envelopes or handmade customized seed packets.

ETIQUETTE

There are a few things to keep in mind before you go to a seed swap.

1. PLANT CHOICE
Bring noninvasive, open-pollinated seeds (see page 18).

2. SEED VIABILITY
Vegetable seeds should be no older than three years, unless they have been properly dried and stored. As they age, seeds are less likely to germinate successfully.

3. PACKAGING AND LABELING
It can be fun making your own seed packets and labels. Make sure you include important information, such as the date, plant name (common and scientific), eventual height and spread, and any growing tips.

4. ORGANIZATION
For ease of exchange, display seeds in boxes categorized by plant type, such as tree, climber, or vegetable.

Tip
Start with fruit/vegetables/flowers that you know you like. Perhaps discuss with the group what seeds everybody would like to eventually have.

SEED ACTIVISM

Seed activism is a global uprising of farmers and gardeners who believe in the freedom to save and share seeds without having to purchase them from major seed companies. Some seed companies engineer plant varieties that produce unviable seeds. These seeds cannot be sown for reliable plants, so the gardener is forced to buy, buy, and buy again.

IDEAS, ACTIVITIES, AND EVENTS

SEEDY SUNDAY, BRIGHTON, ENGLAND

A grassroots event inspired by the antigenetic engineering Seedy Saturday event in Canada, Seedy Sunday is currently the biggest seed swap in the UK. It has been running for eleven years and campaigns against buying seeds from companies selling F1 hybrid seeds (see page 19), which are incapable of producing worthy seeds to use the next year. The Seedy Sunday (www.seedysunday.org) event in Brighton, England, takes place every February and has up to 2,000 seed activists attending workshops and talks, and swapping seeds.

SEED BOMBS

We can't talk about seed activism without mentioning seed bombing! This is a growing phenomenon whereby "guerrilla" gardeners beautify urban wasteland with balls of native wildflowers mixed with water, soil, and clay.

INSPIRATION

Dr. Vandana Shiva, founder of Navdanya (see page 51), is a scientist, environmentalist, activist, visionary, and passionate advocate for seed sovereignty. She campaigns against any technology practiced by large seed companies that seek to use genetically modified plants to produce sterile or unviable seeds, which prevents farmers from saving seeds to plant the following season. Dr. Shiva believes that free seed exchange among farmers and growers is the basis of maintaining biodiversity, food security, and centuries of stories and wisdom. Her work has inspired the initiation of seed libraries and seed swapping around the globe.

ABOVE Seed bombs—seeds mixed with clay, soil, and water—are a great way of sowing seeds in an otherwise barren urban landscapes.

RIGHT The inspirational Vandana Shiva, a passionate advocate of seed saving. Shiva received the Right Livelihood Award in 1993.

ABOVE Seedy Sunday in Brighton, England, attracts seed activists from all over the world.

SEED LIBRARIES

These are lending institutions as opposed to seed banks, which primarily save and preserve seeds. They have been initiated by community groups and individuals who are against the control of our seed supply by seed companies, and they believe in seed sovereignty and protecting biodiversity.

Seed libraries follow the model of lending libraries for books, in that seeds are "checked out" with the intention of growing them. In turn, the seeds that grow from them are returned to the library.

START A SEED LIBRARY

If you are tempted to start your own seed library, try these basic steps below. Also see pages 53–56.

1. Find a group of enthusiasts to run the library. Look online and in community spaces.

2. Find a venue. A well-visited community space, such as a library or community center, will make a good meeting place.

3. Find materials. An unwanted wine cooler or chilled vending machine could be used for keeping well-dried seeds cool and easily accessible.

4. Raise funds. Write to local, nonhybrid seed companies explaining your cause and ask for donations.

5. Advertise. Advertise a seed collection point, asking for seed donations. Give strict guidelines, such as describing which seeds will be accepted and which will not be accepted.

6. Get equipped. Assemble a few stationery items, such as envelopes, rubber stamps for checking seeds in and out, and labels. Use a computer to set up a database of borrowers.

7. Find a sign. Use recycled materials to create an eye-catching seed-saving library sign.

8. Find your borrowers. Create a media buzz using flyers, posters, social media, and a Web site.

"Seeds are the first link in the food chain as well as being the storage place for culture and history, and we have the right to save and share them."

DR. VANDANA SHIVA, FOUNDER OF NAVDANYA

HERITAGE VS. HYBRID SEEDS

Plants will adapt their seeds in order to survive in a world that is always changing and evolving. In nature, this can happen slowly as the climate changes and new threats, such as disease, are introduced. However, humans have developed ways to speed up these natural adaptations.

HERITAGE

This is a term used for plants grown over multiple generations whose seeds are kept "true" by conventional breeding. They are often unavailable or difficult to find in the commercial seed trade because they are not deemed commercially viable. Some heritage varieties have been passed on for hundreds of years, and they usually succeed if they possess a superior virtue, such as flavor, color, or texture. They may lack resistance to certain pests and diseases, but the genetic variety they offer makes them an incredibly important resource that plant breeders may need to draw on in the future. All heritage seeds must be open-pollinated.

WHAT IS OPEN-POLLINATED?

These are varieties that will grow "true" from seed and are pollinated openly by wind and insects. They naturally crossbreed with other closely related plants, and the resulting seeds will not be "true." For example, if a chili pepper crosses with a sweet pepper, the offspring will probably be different from either parent. Open-pollinated plants are often well adapted to their local climate and can create their own "natural" hybrids. Open-pollinated plants are the best for saving seeds, and in most cases, their seeds are the only ones accepted in seed swaps.

ADVANTAGES

- Free seeds are produced from year to year and from generation to generation.
- More stable traits are transferred from one plant generation to the next.
- Heritage plant varieties and a larger gene pool are preserved for future breeding.
- The crop will probably mature over a longer period of time, making excessive bumper crops less likely.
- In many cases, flavor and texture are improved.

DISADVANTAGES

- Varieties will self- and cross-pollinate, which can lead to a loss of certain traits. You will need to intervene to prevent this (by caging or isolation, see page 42) in order to produce "true" seeds.
- "Genetic drift" can happen over time and may make plant varieties "deviate" too far from their accepted standard. Removal of these rogue plants will stop them from pollinating other plants and producing too much variation.

HYBRID

Charles Darwin began the hybrid revolution by suggesting that plants mutate and adapt over time in order to survive, and that any environmentally superior traits are passed on to their offspring. This is called natural selection. Prior to Darwin, however, farmers had been artificially selecting the seeds of their best plants, and over time this resulted in domesticated crops. Native Americans, for example, selected the best ears of corn to plant the following year, selecting the plant with the best qualities. In the 1930s, just as the Depression was beginning to hit the country, farmers in the Midwest first crossed two different types of corn to create an artificial hybrid, and it was the first hybridized seed crop to be marketed extensively in the country. Hybridization will happen in the wild, and it is often seen when two previously isolated plants are brought together, either by natural or by artificial means. For example, the Leyland cypress (known for rapid growth in Great Britain) was the result of a previously unheard-of meeting of two North American conifers (Monterey and Nootka cypress) when they were grown together for the first time in a yard in Wales.

Today, plant breeders hybridize plants all the time in an effort to create a perfect plant with desirable traits. Such a hybrid is given an "F1" status, which means it is the first filial generation of two specific male and female parent varieties. F1 seeds are "superseeds" with specific desirable characteristics from both parents. For example, an F1 hybrid tomato may have the early fruit of one parent and the disease resistance of the other.

Many common vegetables, such as eggplants, tomatoes, melons, and bell peppers are F1 hybrids. These varieties are often selected for their productivity and ability to withstand the long-haul trips to supermarkets. Flavor and variety are often secondary concerns.

RIGHT Corn, so essential to the world's food supply, was the first crop to be hybridized in the United States in the 1930s.

ADVANTAGES

- Wider adaptability to environmental stress.
- Greater uniformity among plants, and higher yields from food crops.
- Improved resistance to pests and diseases.
- Higher survival at the seedling stage.

DISADVANTAGES

- Seeds cannot be saved from year to year because they will not be true to type.
- Their popularity is contributing to the extinction of heritage varieties.
- They lack genetic variety.
- In many cases, the taste of F1 hybrid vegetables and fruit can be bland compared to heritage varieties.
- Breeding is costly and time-consuming, so the seeds are more expensive.
- Patent laws can mean that if the wind accidentally blows patented F1 hybrid seeds onto your land and they grow there, there is a chance you are breaking the law.
- Uniformity of crops means that excessive bumper crops are more likely at harvest time.

GENETICALLY MODIFIED SEEDS

A genetically modified (GM) seed is the offspring of a plant whose genetic characteristics have been altered by the insertion of a modified gene or a gene from another organism through genetic engineering. It is a modern form of plant breeding that bypasses the more traditional methods.

"SEEDS OF DISCONTENT"

Although the methods of genetic modification are different, the aims are the same: to enhance existing desirable traits and to introduce new ones.

Some scientists believe that GM crops will help combat worldwide famine by producing plants with higher tolerances that result in fewer risks of failure. Potentially, genetic engineering is fast and very accurate; for example, by identifying a gene that is responsible for drought tolerance and modifying it, in theory, the desired traits will then be passed on to the offspring.

Genes from nonplant organisms can also be transferred. One famous example is the use of modified genes from a naturally occurring soil bacteria, *Bacillus thuringiensis*, in corn. These genes caused the corn plants to produce crystallized proteins that are lethal to a certain caterpillar pest that feeds on the crops. Plants that contain the *B. thuringiensis* gene are considered safe for human consumption, and safe for the environment, although this is a new science and research and debate is still continuing.

Many people have a strong opinion about GM foods, from environmental activists and religious organizations to scientists, government officials, and the companies that create them. In theory, the science behind GM crops could do a lot of good in the world, from improving the food supply and reducing the use of agrochemicals, but the environmental hazards and the risk to human health posed by GM technology, as well as the vested economic and political interests, are all huge concerns.

RISKS

- Chemicals expressed by GM genes could have an unexpected effect on other organisms, including humans. For example, in the United States, pollen from *B.t.* corn is believed to cause high mortality rates in monarch butterfly caterpillars, which were not the target pest.

- GM plants may create new allergens. For example, a proposal to incorporate a gene from Brazil nuts into soybeans was abandoned in case it caused an allergic reaction when consumed.

- GM crops may cross-pollinate with natural crops and wild relatives, which could lead to widespread genetic contamination. If such genes were engineered for herbicide tolerance, crossing with related weed species might result in herbicide-tolerant "superweeds." Marketing GM foods is lengthy and costly, which could result in consumers paying higher prices for food.

SEED COMPANIES

Seed production is a worldwide multibillion-dollar business. Most seeds are produced by large specialty growers who focus on only a few crop types. The large companies sell wholesale seeds to smaller companies, who then package them into smaller packets to sell to the amateur gardener. More recently, GM crops have been introduced into the picture. Many multinational seed companies have vested interests in this technology, because GM seeds can be patented and potentially offer greater control of the market. Many farmers and gardeners have begun to react to this by reclaiming their rights to grow nonhybrid seeds for saving and swapping.

After the Haiti earthquake in 2010, Monsanto, the world's biggest seed company and market leader in selling GM seeds, donated a $4 million "gift" of 60,000 seed sacks. The hybrid seeds were treated with highly toxic pesticides and needed to be handled with protective gloves. The Ministry of Agriculture rejected Monsanto's offer because concerns were raised that by accepting it, small farmers would enter agreements that may have resulted in being forced to buy Monsanto's expensive seeds each year. Approximately 10,000 Haitian farmers and protesters burned the seeds on June 4, 2010, for World Environment Day (www.foodsafetynews.com).

ABOVE AND TOP GM crops—a new and potentially serious threat to the diversity of our crops.

THE SAFE SEED PLEDGE

"We pledge that we do not knowingly buy or sell genetically engineered seeds or plants."

Before the rise of commercial seed giants, most practiced gardeners and farmers selected and saved seeds from the healthiest plants. These were grown the following year and so on, thus strengthening the strain. This way of gardening guaranteed local adaptation to pests and diseases and ensured genetic diversity. The recent uprising among farmers and ethical seed companies around the world, who believe in seed freedom and sovereignty, has grown into a recognized oath called "The Safe Seed Pledge." The pledge was initiated in 1999 by High Mowing Organic Seeds as a statement about the signers' stand against genetic modification. So far, more than 70 seed companies have signed the pledge. For a list, visit www.councilforresponsiblegenetics.org

SEEDS AND CULTURE

Seeds are the little suitcases that store the evolution of plant species and the culture of their growers. Over thousands of years, cultures have developed a unique cuisine built upon the food crops that grow in their geographical regions. These interconnections between plants, people, and cultures are studied by ethnobotanists.

EARLY SEED SWAPS

The knowledge accumulated by ethnobotanists enables us to see how our forefathers used plants for culinary and medicinal purposes. Plants were exchanged when travelers visited or migrated to different countries, and these exchanges fundamentally changed each culture. When European explorers traveled to the Americas in 1492, crops, such as wheat, onions, garlic, and wine grapes, and herbs, such as cilantro and parsley, were taken with them. Squash, beans, corn, and potatoes were brought back to Europe. Some seeds were intentionally exchanged, and some were unknowingly transported, hidden in nooks and crannies of the ships and dispersed by the elements on arrival. This process carried the risk of transporting alien species that could affect native plants and crops by being invasive and introducing pests and diseases. More positively, it means that seeds that once belonged to a particular country now belong to the world.

FOODS OF YOUR CULTURE

Cultural foods are meaningful. Their smell and taste evoke memories, and some travelers will take the traditional foods of their region on long journeys because they are vital to their diets and have physical and spiritual significance. The demand for traditional vegetables, herbs, and spices has inspired multicultural street markets and some convenience stores to stock unusual and exciting grains, fruit, vegetables, and spices. Those who have emigrated can still cook the food of their culture using traditional herbs and spices.

ABOVE AND BELOW Just like people, seeds and foods pass from one culture to another, enriching the lives and diets of people as they travel. What was once exotic, becomes commonplace.

AN INTRODUCTION
TO SEEDS

SEEDS: THEIR PURPOSE AND IMPORTANCE

Seeds are the source of life. They support our ecosystems and enable flowering plants to avoid extinction. They're also a source of food for humans and animals, in seed and in fruit and vegetable form.

A seed contains an embryo (unborn plant), which is formed in the ovary of a flower. The embryo is surrounded by a protective coat called the testa, that nourishes and prevents the seed from drying out, and protects it from any mechanical injuries that might occur after dispersal.

The sole purpose of a plant is to reproduce. Some plants can reproduce vegetatively, by producing offsets and runners, but in most cases, seed production is the most effective way of ensuring the genetic diversity and long-term success of a species. Seeds are a food source to wildlife (and humans), and many of them won't reach germination because of being eaten, so as insurance, an individual plant can produce tens, hundreds, and even thousands of seeds.

For a flowering plant to produce seeds, it has to work in partnership with nature and adapt in ways that will attract partners, such as insects, bees, butterflies, small mammals, and birds.

Insects help by transferring pollen, thus enabling fertilization so that seeds can form in the ovary. The most effective way of attracting pollinators is by producing colorful flowers with dazzling patterns and seductive scents. The pollinators are rewarded with sweet nectar. Plants that are grown outside of their natural habitat, away from their specific pollinators, usually need introduced pollinators or to be pollinated by hand.

RIGHT This pink campion uses its bright petals to attract insect pollinators. The seed head swells until it reaches maturity. It will dry in the sun and turn brown. The crown peels back to reveal tiny black seeds which will be dispersed by wind.

The shape and size of seeds vary greatly and will depend on their dispersal method. For example, some wind-carried seeds are winged or feathered; others are formed within or on the outside of brightly colored fruit to entice birds and small mammals. Whether they pass through an animal or travel across the skies and the seas, the sole purpose of seeds is to spread themselves as widely as possible. For millennia, humans have played their own important role in seed dispersal by collecting, growing, and storing seeds—a tradition that continues today with seed swapping.

SEED FORMATION

Before a seed can even be formed, the flower has to be pollinated. This can be done by the wind, insects, or artificially by hand. There are male and female reproductive parts of the flower. Most flowers have both, but some flowers are single sex, such as pumpkin flowers. Seed formation is described in more detail on page 26.

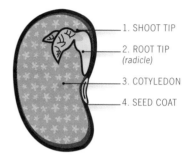

SEED ANATOMY

A typical seed includes these basic parts.

1. SHOOT TIP
2. ROOT TIP *(radicle)*
3. COTYLEDON
4. SEED COAT

REPRODUCTION

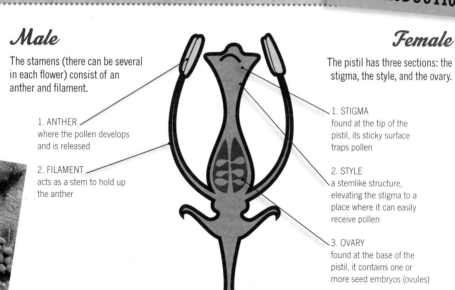

Male

The stamens (there can be several in each flower) consist of an anther and filament.

1. ANTHER
where the pollen develops and is released

2. FILAMENT
acts as a stem to hold up the anther

Female

The pistil has three sections: the stigma, the style, and the ovary.

1. STIGMA
found at the tip of the pistil, its sticky surface traps pollen

2. STYLE
a stemlike structure, elevating the stigma to a place where it can easily receive pollen

3. OVARY
found at the base of the pistil, it contains one or more seed embryos (ovules)

POLLINATION AND FERTILIZATION

Pollination is a significant part of the reproduction process of flowering plants, where pollen is transferred from an anther to a stigma. It enables fertilization and the consequent formation of seeds. Some flowers are able to pollinate themselves (self-pollination), whereas others will only accept pollen from a separate plant.

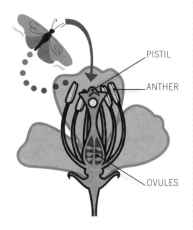

POLLINATION

PISTIL
ANTHER
OVULES

- The stigma traps a grain of pollen, which germinates into a pollen tube and grows down the style and into the ovary.
- The pollen tube reaches an ovule and releases two male cells.
- One cell combines with the ovule; the second combines with the polar nuclei and later becomes the endosperm (food supply).
- Fertilization occurs.
- Once the ovule, or ovules, have been fertilized, the flower is no longer needed, and the petals and stamens will wither.
- Seed maturity can take about 25 to 30 days.
- The fertilized ovule develops into an embryo contained within the seed.
- Ovules are white at the time of fertilization and eventually turn pale green as the seed enlarges during its early stages of development.
- Each seed is attached to the ovary wall by a stalk, from which it receives the food to fuel its growth.
- As the seeds develop, the ovary enlarges, becoming recognizable as a fruit or seed pod.

The development of the fruit differs from plant to plant; some seeds develop within a wet fruit, such as an eggplant or tomato, and some develop within a dry seed pod, such as a poppy seed head or pea pod.

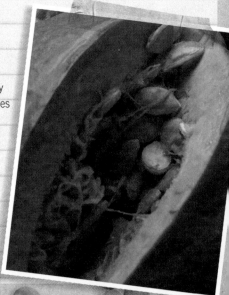

RIGHT Some seeds, such as pumpkin seeds, are wet, and others, such as peas, are dry seeds.

HAND-POLLINATION

In hand-pollination, people intervene to control the pollination process. This may simply be because there are no pollinators present (if, for example, plants are grown in a greenhouse), but usually the purpose is to enable the parent plants to produce "true" seeds. Gardeners can transfer pollen from the anthers to the stigma, using a small soft brush or a cotton swab. For self-pollinating plants, gardeners can shake the plants, which loosens the pollen and allows for it to be transferred in the air, or they can simply rub together the flowers. There are varying methods that have been developed for specific plants. Two methods are described here:

CURCUBIT TECHNIQUE

Curcubits, such as cucumbers and pumpkins, have separate male and female flowers on the same plant. At the bottom of the female flower is an ovary that resembles an undeveloped fruit. The male flower lacks this feature, simply having a thin stalk. To keep your seeds "true," follow these steps:

1. Before dusk, locate male and female flowers from the same plant.

2. To prevent insects from flying in, use masking tape to shut the tips of the flowers that are about to open the next morning.

3. When the morning dew has dried the following day, pluck off the male flower, leaving a short stem. Gently remove the tape and all the petals, leaving only the anthers. The male flower is now a pollen paintbrush!

4. Carefully remove the tape from the female flower and let it open. Swipe the pollen brush onto the female stigma.

5. Retape the female flower and securely mark the stem with colorful waterproof string.

6. The eventual fruit will be the one from which you save your "true" seeds.

RIGHT You need to cover the flower heads before they open to prevent bees from pollinating the sunflowers.

SUNFLOWER TECHNIQUE

1. Cover two flower heads with a separate porous bag before the florets open to prevent them from being accessed by pollinating insects.

2. Seal them around the flower stalks with tape. When the flowers start shedding pollen, remove one of the bags and gently rub the flower head with a soft brush.

3. Remove the bag from the other flower head, and use the same brush to brush another flower.

4. Replace the bags around the flower heads swiftly after pollinating to exclude the chance of any additional pollination by insects or birds.

5. The florets open in succession, so brush the same flower heads daily for up to two weeks.

GERMINATION

Germination is a process by which the embryo of a plant grows from the seed stage to the seedling stage. Three factors must be fulfilled before a seed will germinate:

1. Seed viability The embryo must be alive.

2. Seed dormancy Dormancy must be overcome; some seeds will remain dormant (asleep) until they have experienced certain conditions, such as being passed through the digestive system of an animal or going through a period of cold, soaking, scarification, or fermentation.

3. Environmental conditions These include oxygen, temperature, light, and water.

THE PHASES

As a seed germinates, it goes through three phases before it sprouts into a seedling.

1. Water imbibition Water triggers germination. The embryo within the seed absorbs water, which causes it to swell until the testa bursts.

2. The lag phase The cells prepare for growth, adjusting to the environment but not yet actively dividing.

3. Radicle emergence The stage in which the seedling root (radicle) emerges from the seed.

Radicle emergence is considered the completion of germination, and the plant then moves toward the seedling stage.

VIABILITY

In seed terms, the definition of viability is "the potential to germinate." The length a seed stays viable varies from plant to plant, but correct storage conditions can increase its chances of successful future germination.

ABOVE You can see the emerging radicle on these lentil seeds.

BELOW As soon as the seed leaves rise, they begin to photosynthesize, which helps fuel the growth of these little seedlings.

The oldest recorded seed to be germinated was from a Judean date palm, resurrected in 2005 from a 2,000-year-old seed at the Louis L. Borick Natural Medicine Research Center, Israel.

Some seeds have an extended longevity, enabling them to exist in the "soil seed bank" for many years before the right conditions present themselves for germination.

DORMANCY

A seed remains dormant to make sure of minimal risk of failure. It is a way of enduring until conditions are optimal for germination and the survival of the seedling. Dormancy will not be broken if conditions are too dark or too light, too hot or cold, or too dry. It will only break if the conditions are just right: when the soil is moist enough and the temperature is correct. For example, some plants from arid parts of the world and some grasses need a period of low moisture and will only germinate after a period of drying.

Not all seeds, even if they are of the same cultivar, break their dormancy at exactly the same time. This is a fairly common adaptation, which enables plants to avoid any potential threats, such as a late frost or being eaten. It is nature's way of making sure some seedlings survive.

DORMANCY TYPES

Morphological Here, the embryo is underdeveloped at dispersal. Germination will be prevented until the embryo is fully developed.

Physiological Chemical inhibitors prevent the embryo from breaking through the seed coat. Dormancy will only break when external environmental factors, such as sunlight or high temperatures, cause these inhibitors to break down.

Morphophysiological These seeds have underdeveloped embryos and physiological restraints. They may need dormancy-breaking treatments, such as stratification, scarification, or soaking.

Physical This is when the seed coats are hard, making them impermeable to water. The seed may need to undergo some kind of physical or chemical process before dormancy is broken, such as passing through an animal's digestive system.

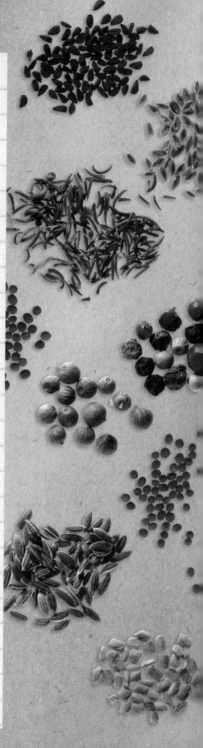

DISPERSAL

Plants adapt to where they are growing, and fruits come in many shapes and sizes to disperse their seeds efficiently.

EDIBLE

Delicious fruits entice animals, such as mammals and birds, to eat the fruit and, thus, carry the seeds in their stomachs. As the seed is being digested, seed-growth inhibitors and the hard seed coats are degraded. The seed is excreted and ready to germinate in a pile of nutritious fertilizer, ideally some distance away from where it was originally picked up.

EXPLOSIVE

As they dry, some fruits explode, expelling their seeds. For example, some bean pods build a tension as they dry, eventually releasing like a spring, which can flick the seeds away.

HITCHHIKING

Some seeds develop sticky hooks or spines in order to attach to clothing or fur and hitch a ride on passing animals and humans. Burs are typical examples, and they are said to have inspired the invention of Velcro.

WATER

Plants that grow by the water rely on it to carry seeds to new locations. The fruit will have to be waterproof and buoyant, and a classic example is the coconut, which successfully travels long distances across the ocean. It will either germinate in the water or when it eventually lodges in a muddy bank or sandy beach.

WIND

Shaped so the wind can carry them off, some seeds have wings or feathery parts to their anatomy. The propeller-like "keys" of maples and the feathery "parachutes" of dandelions are typical examples.

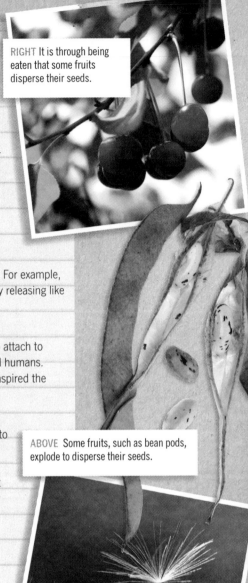

RIGHT It is through being eaten that some fruits disperse their seeds.

ABOVE Some fruits, such as bean pods, explode to disperse their seeds.

RIGHT Light-as-a-feather dandelion seeds are dispersed by wind.

THE BENEFITS
OF SWAPPING

SAVING BY SAVING

Money is tight and times are tough, so why not cut some of your costs by saving and swapping seeds? Using your seeds as currency to gain additional seeds can save considerably, and a successful seed circle will mean you'll never have to buy seeds again!

SEED CIRCLE MATH

- If fifteen savers each save two different vegetables, the results will be thirty packets of seeds each.
- An average packet of seeds costs $3.95, so that's a saving of $118.50 per year.
- Store them and grow two different vegetables next season.
- By the third year of your seed circle, everyone will have ninety packets of different seeds.

TIME SAVING AND STOCKING UP

The benefits of saving and swapping seeds are not only financial, they may also help you save time. If someone else grows the plant the first time around, you will get the benefit of his or her experience. You can stock up on time-saving growing tips and ways to avoid potential disasters. The best thing about community seed sharing and swapping is that any experience earned will be specific to your local growing conditions, and the chance to pool all the combined knowledge from your community is invaluable to your gardening experience.

Seed swapping is an "exchange" and an opportunity to pass on any helpful tips and techniques about the seeds you swap. These should be passed on, either on the seed packet or on an attached note.

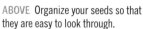

ABOVE Organize your seeds so that they are easy to look through.

PUMPKIN

DATE COLLECTED . . .

This plant was handed down to me from my grandmother in Boston

Tip

Remember to use only open-pollinated seeds for your seed circle, so they will produce plants with viable seeds to pass on that are "true" to type.

ENVIRONMENTAL BENEFITS

COMMUNITY

Seed swapping strengthens community links. It's a great way of making new friends, and there will probably be many interesting conversations you can join. At seed swaps, there are often talks and workshops on related subjects, such as beekeeping, wildflowers, rare plants, biodiversity, and even how to cook with your home produce.

FOOD DIVERSITY

Conserving seeds is conserving food diversity and a wide range of crops. It took 10,000 years to develop the agricultural diversity we enjoy today, and this is being threatened by global food industries whose single aim is profit. As a result, we have hyperproductive, hyperdurable plant varieties in place of organically grown, open-pollinated plants.

Food diversity is plummeting into a world of monocropping. The seed-saving community is seed activism at its best, a worldwide group effort to preserve plant diversity.

WILDLIFE

Saving seeds saves species. Plant diversity supports wildlife diversity, and together they create the healthy ecosystem that is fundamental to the existence of all living things. The U.S. Fish and Wildlife Service estimates that losing just one plant species can trigger the loss of up to thirty other insect, plant, and animal species.

FOOD SECURITY

Seed savers sow the seeds of food security by growing and eating their own produce. This means that their produce doesn't have far to travel from plot to plate, and gardeners have control over which foods they grow to suit their culture and diet. Being able to save seeds from your own garden secures a food supply for you, for future generations of your family, and for the community with which you seed swap.

ABOVE These perspex rods holding seeds formed part of the Seed Cathedral, built for the 2010 World Expo in Shanghai.

ABOVE AND BELOW Home-grown heritage vegetables are one way in which individuals are helping to preserve food diversity.

BANKING ON SEED COLLECTIONS

Are we banking on the fact that our food reserves will always be here?

Pioneers, such as Nikolai Vavilov, paved the way for the contemporary seed banks and collections. The son of a merchant in Moscow, he was born in 1887. He became a prominent Soviet botanist, geneticist, and one of the world's first scientists to raise international awareness of the need to conserve plants.

The poor rural village in which he grew up was plagued by crop failure and rationing. This fueled his passion for ending famine, and his whole life was devoted to studying and improving the cereal crops that sustain the global population. He studied at Moscow Agricultural Institute, where he wrote his dissertation on snails and plant pests. He studied plant immunity in Europe and organized botanical-agronomic expeditions to collect seeds from around the globe, which were stored in a seed bank in Leningrad. The resulting seed bank eventually contained 400,000 seeds, roots, and fruits. It was, at the time, the world's largest collection of plant seeds.

ABOVE Nikolai Vavilov (1887–1943), a prominent Soviet scientist and one of the first plant conservationists.

The 900-day siege of Leningrad (September 8, 1941, to January 27, 1944) posed a threat to the seed bank. Convinced that Hitler had his sights set on the seeds so he could control the world's food supply, Vavilov's scientists boxed up a range of seeds and hid them in the basement. They guarded them in shifts, and though facing starvation, they refused to eat the seeds because they belonged to the "future." Unfortunately, twelve of the self-appointed seed guardians died of malnourishment while protecting the seeds.

On August 6, 1940, Vavilov was arrested for allegedly destroying Soviet agriculture. He died of malnutrition in a prison in 1943, but after giving more than 100 hours of science lectures. A collection of 200,000 seeds from the Soviet Union and from abroad was seized by a German SS squad in 1943 and partly relocated to the SS Institute for Plant Genetics, which had been set up at Lannach Castle in Austria. The seeds are still missing but it is believed that some of them ended up in Sweden, England, and Argentina.

ABOVE Soviet farmers in 1929, a year in which many poor rural areas experienced crop failure.

SEED DIVERSITY

Seed-bearing plants are grouped into two different divisions: angiosperms and gymnosperms. Angiosperms have "enclosed seeds," in that the seeds are protected inside an ovary. Angiosperms are flowering plants and are the largest group of plants, making up 90 percent of all plant species. The seeds are produced in a fruit, which often helps with seed dispersal. Flowers have been the major success of angiosperms, enabling them to employ the activities of animal visitors to help with their breeding. Gymnosperms have "naked seeds," in that the seeds lie uncovered on the surface of a scale. The largest group of gymnosperms are the conifers, which include pines, cedars, spruces, gingkos, and firs.

THE WORLD'S SMALLEST SEED

This seed is borne by certain epiphytic (tree-dwelling) orchids that grow in tropical rain forests. They produce dustlike seeds that are about three-thousandth of an inch (85 μm) long.

THE WORLD'S LARGEST SEED

This seed is produced by the double coconut palm, *Lodoicea maldivica*. The seeds grow up to 12 inches (30 cm) long and can weigh 40 pounds (18 kg).

CROP DIVERSITY

The loss of crop diversity and the vulnerability of the world's seed collections has been a concern among scientists for many years. Worldwide agriculture relies on about 150 crops, and each crop has a vast range of forms, habits, and tolerances; however, the wild relatives of crops are under threat from the effects of climate change, and so the need to conserve our seed diversity has never been greater. Seed saving is one way to preserve seed and plant diversity for future generations.

> *"Seeds are the source of life."*
> SATISH KUMAR, PEACE AND ENVIRONMENTAL ACTIVIST

ABOVE The largest of the world's seeds, from the double coconut palm, can grow to 12 inches (30 cm) long.

SEED-SWAPPING ORGANIZATIONS

INTERNATIONAL SEEDSAVING INSTITUTE
IDAHO
A nonprofit, educational organization focusing on helping people become self-reliant. www.seedsave.org

THE NATIONAL GARDENING ASSOCIATION
VERMONT
Provides for two-way swaps as well as a forum to post your "wish lists" and lists of seeds to trade. www.garden.org/seedswap

NATIVE SEEDS
ARIZONA
The regional seed bank and leader of the heritage seed movement, promoting ancient crops and their wild relatives by gathering, documenting, safeguarding, and distributing to farming/gardening communities. Their mantra is "returning the seeds of grandparents to people who seek them, and to make available to everyone this wondrous gift, the delicious joy of seeds." www.nativeseeds.org

THE SEED AMBASSADORS PROJECT
OREGON
Initiated by a group of "seed stewards" devoted to seeds. They travel around Europe, learning about seeds and exchanging knowledge to bring back to their farm, where they grow, save, and swap heritage seeds. www.seedambassadors.org

SEED SAVERS EXCHANGE
IOWA
Known for their seed-swapping catalog of thousands of vegetable and fruits. www.seedsavers.org

SOUTHERN SEED LEGACY PROJECT
TEXAS
Strives to preserve plant genetic diversity and cultural knowledge in South America by supporting local seed-saving and exchange networks as well as local conservation. www.pacs.unt.edu/southernseedlegacy

SEEDS OF DIVERSITY
CANADA
A volunteer organization active in conserving the biodiversity and traditional knowledge of food crops and garden plants. www.seeds.ca/en.php

PELITI ALTERNATIVE COMMUNITY GREECE
Founded by Panagiotis Sainatoudis in the remote valley of Mesohori, Peliti collects, distributes, and aims to preserve Greece's traditional varieties. The community has celebrated its twelfth annual "Pan-Hellenic Festival for the exchange of local cultivar seeds." www.peliti.gr

THE GLOBAL CROP DIVERSITY TRUST ITALY
Aims to ensure the worldwide conservation and availability of crop diversity for food security. www.croptrust.org

PRIMAL SEEDS
UNITED KINGDOM
An information network promoting seed saving and swapping, and supporting grassroots movements around the world. www.primalseeds.org

DYFI VALLEY SEED SAVERS WALES/ UNITED KINGDOM
A nonprofit seed-swapping and seed-saving organization. www.dyfivalleyseedsavers.org.uk

SEEDSWAPS
A free, seed-trading Web site www.seedswaps.com

SOURCING AND
SAVING SEEDS

WHERE TO SOURCE SEEDS

Sourcing seeds from your local community is ideal, because plants adapt so well to where they are growing. Seed swaps or asking your neighbors if they have any surplus seeds is a good start, but sometimes this isn't possible so stores and garden centers will be your next port of call.

However, even though they are the closest, they may not be the best places to shop, because the seeds on their shelves may have come from far away, and worse, may not have been stored properly and may not have good germination rates. If you have to go to your local garden center, find the manager and ask him about the seeds. Below are some good Web sites. They are usually happy to offer advice.

SUSTAINABLE SEEDS UNITED STATES
Having taken the "Safe Seed Pledge," this company strives to enrich people's lives through community. It sells its own-grown heritage seeds and seeds from small organic seed farmers. In the company's own words, they are "promoting self-sufficiency through food independence." www.sustainableseedco.com

HEIRLOOM SEEDS UNITED STATES
A small, family-run seed house selling seeds grown by backyard gardeners, whose families have saved the seeds for generations throughout the United States, Canada, Mexico, and overseas. Their seeds meet or exceed federal standards. www.heirloomseeds.com

THE REAL SEED CATALOGUE UNITED KINGDOM
This is an online catalogue of heritage and heritage varieties of vegetable seeds grown with the home gardener and the promotion of seed saving in mind. www.realseeds.co.uk

LUNAR ORGANICS UNITED KINGDOM
How to garden following the phases of the moon, with open-pollinated, heritage, biodynamic seeds. www.lunarorganics.com

ASSOCIATION KOKOPELLI FRANCE
Certified by Ulase, Nature et Progres, and the Soil Association, this is a nonprofit organization working with European farmers and growers of open-pollinated heritage seeds "for the liberation of seed and soil." www.kokopelli-seeds.com

ABOVE Organize your seeds well and swappers get exactly what they need.

MAGIC GARDEN SEEDS GERMANY
A small seed company based in Bavaria, which specializes in open-pollinated heritage, ethnobotanical seeds. www.magicgardenseeds.com

ROYAL HORTICULTURAL SOCIETY UNITED KINGDOM
One of the many benefits of belonging to this society is the opportunity to join their seed distribution plan. Every year, they harvest seeds from hundreds of different plant varieties from their own four gardens. They only distribute to addresses in the European Union, as well as Iceland, Croatia, Norway, and Switzerland. www.rhs.org.uk

WHAT TO LOOK FOR
Before buying seeds, consider what to grow. Choose vegetables that your family enjoys eating and some unusual ones to try out. Measure out your growing space, estimate how tall and wide the crops will be, and find out whether or not they will thrive in your soil and site.

GUIDELINES FOR BUYING SEEDS
The Internet has a wealth of information and Web sites, but it's important to make sure you get your seeds from a good source and that they have been harvested and stored properly. There is a risk that you might buy from a novice who sells you diseased, damaged, poorly stored, or dead seeds.

Before buying, ask these questions:
- **How have the seeds been stored before sale?** If a seed packet has been sitting for months on a shelf in a hot garden center, or in someone's damp shed, it will contain seeds of poor quality. Seeds are living organisms and need to be stored at the correct temperature and humidity to maintain viability.
- **Where are they grown?** Foreign-grown seeds are unlikely to suit your growing conditions, and the plants may struggle in your garden as a result. Try to make sure you buy seeds of relatively local origin.
- **Are they an F1 hybrid?** If you want to save seeds that are "true" to type, you must find out if the seeds are open-pollinated.

Keep records of where you got your seeds from, how many you ordered, and how much they were. This information can be a useful resource for future purchases.

ABOVE A member of the Curcubit family, achocha seeds are said to have been grown by the ancient Inca in South America as a food crop.

BELOW You can pass on any surplus seeds that you have purchased that are fit for swapping.

SHELF LIFE

As soon as seeds are harvested, they begin to age, and if they aren't stored properly, they are at risk of dying or losing vigor. Aged seeds may be slow to germinate or they may fail to germinate at all. Sometimes they produce abnormal seedlings.

The "shelf life" (longevity) of seeds varies from plant to plant. Some are short-lived, but most are capable of surviving for many years under the optimum storage conditions. Scientists from Kew's Millennium Seed Bank at Wakehurst Place in England have been conducting comparative seed longevity experiments where seeds are "aged" to develop a ranking category. They have discovered that seeds with an endosperm (and so with relatively smaller embryos) from plants that grow in cool, moist environments are more likely to have a shorter life than nonendospermic seeds (with relatively larger embryos) that come from warmer, drier regions.

In the fall of 1879, Dr. William James Beal, then professor of botany and forestry at Michigan Agricultural College, initiated a seed viability experiment, which is the longest-running experiment on seed longevity. He prepared twenty lots and selected fifty fresh seeds from twenty-three different plants. The seeds were mixed with moderately moist sand and placed in uncorked bottles, which were buried 3 feet (0.9 m) deep with the mouth slanted downward, so water couldn't accumulate around the seeds. The bottles were laid out in rows and buried in a sandy hilltop near the college on unplowed land. Every five years a bottle was dug up, and its contents mixed with soil in seed flats and tested for germination.

After forty years, amaranth (*Amaranthus*) germinated successfully, followed by *Oenothera, Brassica,* and *Rumex crispus*. The fifteenth bottle was recovered on April 22, 2000, after being buried for 120 years. Twenty-three seeds of *Verbascum blattaria* and two seeds of a different *Verbascum* species germinated and produced normal plants, and a single seed of *Malva rotundifolia* germinated after six week's cold treatment. Five more bottles were left buried.

ABOVE All aspects of seed development are studied by scientists at Kew's Millennium Seed Bank in England.

ABOVE In an experiment, amaranth germinated from forty-year-old seeds.

TIPS AND TECHNIQUES

Remember that seeds stored in an open container will absorb moisture from the air, promoting aging, germination, and possibly rotting.

When is a seed dry enough to store? Some farmers mix equal amounts of salt and seeds in a glass jar, shake it, and let it sit for 20 minutes. If the seeds are still wet, the salt absorbs their moisture and will stick to the sides of the jar. Scientists at Kew's Millennium Seed Bank at Wakehurst Place use digital hygrometers, which measure the air surrounding the seed after 30 minutes in a sealed chamber. These give an accurate reading of the equilibrium relative humidity (eRH). For short-term storage, a reading of below 70 percent eRH is acceptable, but 15 percent eRH is recommended for long-term storage, preferably under cold conditions. Some cheaper alternatives, such as self-indicating silica gel and moisture-indicating strips, are available online or from specialty suppliers.

Temperature The shelf life of seeds decreases if temperatures are high. Ideally, the storage temperature should be -4°F (-20°C). The Millennium Seed Bank suggests that for every 9°F (13°C) reduction in temperature, seed longevity will double.

Ambient drying In many countries, the sun is used to dry out seeds, which are traditionally laid out on a tarpaulin and shuffled occasionally. Alternatively, you can dry seeds in porous bags in crates, raised off the floor to improve air circulation. For small-scale seed saving, the humble paper bag is perfectly acceptable.

Rice dry Rice draws the moisture from your seeds. Bake the rice for 45 minutes, and while still hot pour into a large glass jar and screw the lid on, waiting for the rice to cool. Add your seeds to a porous bag—for example, a paper bag or one made from some old cotton socks—tie shut, and place on top of the rice. Tighten the lid and store in a cool, dry, dark place for two weeks. After this, the seeds should be dry enough to be stored in an airtight container.

Instant milk If you often open the container to use your seeds, moisture can seep in. To keep your seeds dry, you can make a pocket from a sheet of paper towel and fill it with instant milk powder. Secure the pocket shut with a paper clip and let it sit in your seed container for up to six months.

> ### *Tip*
> When the seeds have been air dried, they can be dried even more with a drying agent, such as rice. Use a ratio of three parts of desiccant for every one part of seeds.

BELOW Adding a pocket of instant milk to your seeds will help draw moisture away.

SEED-SAVING TECHNIQUES

These techniques will help to make sure the seeds you save are "true," which means that they have not cross-pollinated with others in their species or wild relatives, resulting in physical deformities. It is important that seeds are dried and stored in such a way to be sure of successful germination.

ISOLATION AND CAGING
These are ways to prevent cross-pollination.

ISOLATION
The isolation distance must be far enough to prevent pollen from being carried by the wind and visiting insects—it varies from species to species. For example, eggplants can be isolated by just 16 yards (15 m), whereas beets need at least 5 miles (8 km). Isolating varieties may be a difficult thing to accomplish if you live in a built-up area and your neighbor is growing plants of the same species. Consequently, isolation isn't effective for urban areas, unless you are growing uncommon plants.

TIME ISOLATION
Annual varieties can be isolated by time. Separate the flowering periods by planting two varieties with different maturity rates, such as an early crop and a late crop. Plant the first crop as early as possible, and just before the first crop flowers you can sow the next cultivar. This works well with crops such as cilantro, sunflower, corn, and lettuce.

BAGGING FLOWERS
Bagging is a method used for self-pollinating plants, such as tomatoes and eggplants, but excluding corn. By covering flowers with porous bags made from spun polyester, you are creating a barrier so the insects can't get in. Tie the bags around individual flower heads or groups. Make sure there are no gaps around the stems for insects to crawl into. Shake the plants occasionally to disperse the pollen from flower to flower, and when the fruits have formed, remove the bag and mark the plant as being the one from which you can save seeds.

ABOVE Wild carrot is a common weed that will cross-pollinate with your vegetable carrots.

ABOVE Winnowing peanuts in Madagascar.

CAGING

Pollination cages can be used for both self- and insect-pollinated plants. Cover them with spun polyester or fine net curtains. These net cages need to have good airflow, let in water and light, and keep insects out. Low-growing crops can be caged by using bendy poles or semicircular wire pushed into the ground. Bigger crop cages can be made from wood or plastic pipes. Make sure the fabric is buried under the soil to prevent any insect squatters.

Introducing pollinators into your cages is essential for insect-pollinated plants. Honeybees can be lured inside by placing a plate of honey beside the cage.

ALTERNATE DAY CAGING

You can grow a number of different cultivars of the same plant in your garden. Remove the cage from one cultivar each day (replace the cage in the evening) to let it be naturally pollinated by insects without the risk of crossing with the other caged cultivars.

HAND-POLLINATION

This allows for you to transfer pollen from flower to flower by hand to prevent cross-pollination (see page 27).

THRESHING AND WINNOWING

Threshing and winnowing is a dry-seed processing technique that separates the seeds from the chaff.

THRESHING

The seeds are released from their coverings by rubbing, beating, or flailing. Whole seed heads can be placed in a pillowcase and gently trampled on, or smaller seeds can be carefully mashed between two wooden boards.

WINNOWING

Used to separate the smaller chaff from seeds, one method is to toss seeds from a basket. This allows for the wind to separate the lighter debris from the heavier seeds. However, a sudden gust of wind could take your whole seed collection with it. An alternative to wind is to use a household fan or an old hair dryer with the heating element taken out. Cover the area you are winnowing with a sheet to catch any stray seeds.

DRY SEEDS AND WET SEEDS

Different seeds require different harvesting and saving techniques. Some plants set seed after one growing season, but others need more planning, such as biennial vegetables, including carrots and onions. These need two growing seasons and a period of cold before they set seed. Some seeds are released from the plant only when the seed head or pod has dried, and these include such plants as corn, beans, and carrots. Other seeds are contained within a fleshy "fruit," such as tomatoes and zucchini, and will need extraction methods, such as scraping out and soaking, and for germinating in the short term, they may need fermenting.

RIGHT Remember to store seeds only when they are completely dry.

DRY SEEDS

Dry seeds are not hidden within a fleshy fruit. Usually when the flower has died, the petals fall away or turn brown, and the seed head or pod will form and swell. Collect the seeds on a sunny day when they feel dry and before the seed head breaks open or is eaten by birds.

Allocate a paper bag or pillowcase and label it with the plant you are collecting from to avoid mixing up the seeds.

Cut off the seed heads or pods with up to 8 inches (20 cm) of stem, and place them, head down, in the bag. Tie the bag closed around the stems and hang it up in a well-ventilated, dry place indoors for up to three weeks.

It is relatively simple to separate the seeds from the chaff with dry seeds, because the seeds tend to be released as the seed head dries. Threshing and winnowing may be required (see page 43).

RIGHT An assortment of dry seeds I collected from my garden. It is important to know what they are before you mix them up like this and to separate the seeds before you dry and store them.

Tip

Make sure your seeds are cleaned and dried properly before you bank them or they might rot in storage. Wet seeds, such as cucumber, and larger seeds, such as beans and peas, may take longer to dry out.

WET SEEDS

Wet seeds, such as cucumber and squash, are embedded within a fleshy body and need to be separated from the flesh before you dry them. Some of these fruits and vegetables, such as zucchini, are deliberately harvested when young for consumption, but they need to continue to grow for several more weeks before the seeds will be ripe for collection.

SEPARATING THE SEEDS FROM THE PULP

Large fruits and vegetables, such as pumpkin, are usually chopped open, and the seeds are scraped out with a spoon. They are then sieved and pulled apart under running water from a faucet.

Seeds from small fruits or vegetables, such as tomatoes, need to be lightly mashed out with the juices into a bowl and washed and sieved repeatedly until they are clean.

Wet seeds will stick to porous items, such as paper, so they should be laid out evenly over a labeled ceramic plate or drying screen for a number of days in a dry spot. Shuffle and turn the seeds occasionally to prevent them from sticking to each other or rotting.

When the seeds are properly dry, store them in a labeled, airtight container.

For germinating in the short term, some wet seeds can undergo the fermenting process (see page 46).

RIGHT Wet seeds need to be scraped out of the flesh.

ABOVE Sieve and wash seeds thoroughly.

Tip

Remember it is important to wait for the seeds to mature on the plant before you harvest them. This applies just as much to wet seeds as it does to dry seeds. For wet seeds, let the flesh overripen, and for dry seeds, let the seeds change color (in most cases), harden, and loosen on the seed head.

RIGHT Dry seeds completely before storing.

FERMENTATION

Fermentation occurs as a natural process in the garden as the fruits fall to the ground and rot, or are passed through the digestive system of an animal. Fermentation kills off any seed-borne diseases that can affect the next generation of plants and improves the ability to sprout by degrading growth inhibitors. Only ferment seeds that you will probably germinate in the short term, that is, within five years. The fermentation process is not suitable if you want to store seeds for longer than this because you don't want to degrade the growth inhibitors.

The fermentation process can easily be mimicked in the kitchen. Scoop out the seeds and pulp into a jar and fill it with double the amount of water. Stir vigorously and store the mixture in a warm place at 86°F (30°C) for up to three days until you see white bubbling on the surface of the mixture. After a day of bubbling, pour the brew into a bowl of water and gently separate the seeds from the pulp with your fingers. Live seeds will sink to the bottom of the bowl. Rinse and sieve several times, then place the seeds on a plate in a cool, dry place for several days before storing them in an airtight container.

It is questionable as to whether the fermentation process helps or hinders seeds that you want to store in the long term, because the growth inhibitors keep the seed dormant and will probably degrade over time in long-term storage anyway. I suggest that during the cleaning process, you put a batch aside without fermentation to be on the safe side.

ABOVE It may not look pretty, but fermentation stops disease from passing from one generation to the next.

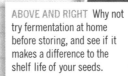

ABOVE AND RIGHT Why not try fermentation at home before storing, and see if it makes a difference to the shelf life of your seeds.

SEED BANKS

THE BIG PICTURE

Plants are fundamental for the welfare of human society and for the function of our ecosystem. They provide us with oxygen, medicine, fiber for clothing, material to build with, and, most important, food. Have you ever wondered what would happen if plants vanished?

Consumption is exceeding production, the world's supplies of natural resources are dwindling, and farmers are under constant pressure to increase yields in order to keep up. There has never been a more critical time to try to protect what we have, and scientists have found a solution: seed banks.

WHY BANK SEEDS?

Historians believe that agriculture began as far back as 8000 B.C.E. in Mesopotamia, and harvesting was one of the most important events in the calendars of ancient farming communities. Farmers could have needed to protect their seeds from animals and extreme weather to save seeds for next year's harvest.

RIGHT AND BELOW Drought and flooding can be seen as a result of climate change, and both endanger food supplies.

These days the need to save seed remains as vital as ever; in fact, the reasons for doing so have multiplied:

- Climate change is causing global weather patterns to change, which can lead to habitat loss and extinction of important species.
- Natural and man-made disasters can wipe out whole farming communities, and seeds from global seed banks can help farmers to recover quickly. This is what happened after the tsunami in 2004, when rice paddies were obliterated in Malaysia and Sri Lanka.
- Overcollection of plants from the wild, particularly those needed for construction materials, food, or for their medicinal value, can mean that they are threatened with extinction.

If we continue the way we are, it is estimated that a species a day will be lost over the next fifty years.

WHICH SEEDS GET BANKED?

Scientists are attempting to make a "Noah's Ark" of all seeds. Some banks, however, focus their efforts on storing indigenous wildflowers, while some focus on specialty vegetables. Others have a more global focus and select crops deemed to be "globally beneficial," such as rice, potatoes, oats, barley, legumes, bananas, carrots, and corn.

THE SEED BANK PROCESS:
- Species are chosen and located, with the actual seed collection done by global partners or seed bank staff.
- Collection occurs manually with hand tools and buckets or bags.
- A pressed plant specimen is also collected with the seeds to add to the seed bank's herbarium.
- Each collection is assigned a unique number and has a record card with details, such as the collector's name, location, habitat, plant name, soil type, and how it was processed.
- The seeds are cleaned by shaking them through a hand sieve or passing them through an aspirator.
- The collection is dried in porous bags at a controlled temperature of 59°F (15°C) and 15 percent relative humidity for up to a week. The seeds are stored in labeled airtight containers at -4°F (-20°C).

Some seeds may need cryopreservation, where they are stored in liquid nitrogen, and some plants whose seeds do not store well may need to be stored in vitro; this is where living plant tissues are stored in liquid nitrogen to make sure of efficient long-term storage. Seeds with a short storage life need to be replanted, harvested, and rebanked at set intervals.

ABOVE Scientists from all over the world are engaged in collecting seeds for our future.

RIGHT The need to conserve seeds is becoming more and more urgent.

GLOBAL SEED BANKS

There are currently about 1,400 seed banks in the world. They operate in a similar way to savings accounts—seeds are deposited into the bank to draw from at a later date.

SAVING OUR SEEDS SEED BANK UNITED STATES

Provides information, resources, and publications for gardeners, farmers, seed savers, and seed growers. The seed bank project aims to rescue and preserve seeds, in particular family heritage seeds. It is seeking seed donations and stories or family histories that come with the seeds. www.savingourseeds.org

THE CHEROKEE NATION UNITED STATES

This organization has been building a seed bank of Cherokee heirloom crops for many years. By taking action to preserve their genetically pure, ancient, staple crop cultivars, which have been grown by the Cherokee people for thousands of years, they are handing down their traditional dietary, medicinal, and gardening skills for future generations. www.cherokeeatlarge.org

SEED SAVERS EXCHANGE UNITED STATES

Founded in 1975, this organization dedicates an 890-acre heritage farm to its nonprofit seed-saving and learning-through workshops. It has banked many thousands of heritage seeds that were brought to North America by its members, whose ancestors emigrated from diverse parts of the world, such as Europe, the Middle East, and Asia. www.seedsavers.org

UNIVERSIDAD POLITÉCNICA DE MADRID SEED BANK (UPM) SPAIN

This seed bank was initiated in 1966 by Professor César Gómez-Campo (1933–2009) at the Technical University of Madrid. Devoted to wild species, it was the first of its kind in the world and pioneered seed banking of wild species and seed storing. An example of its success lies with the species *Diplotaxis siettiana*, a flowering plant in the Brassicaceae (cabbage) family that grew exclusively on the Spanish island of Alboran and disappeared in 1985. Fortunately, the UPM seed bank had stored some seeds in 1974, which saved the species from extinction. www.upm.es

ABOVE A simple seed storage system in a home in Brazil.

ABOVE A man keeps a seed bank in his home in northern Ethiopia—some seed banks are purely local affairs.

SVALBARD GLOBAL SEED VAULT NORWAY

Also known as the "Doomsday Vault," this seed vault opened
for storage in February 2008. It is located deep in the side of a
frozen arctic mountain in Longyearbyen, Norway, about 800 miles
(1,300 km) from the North Pole. It is a global backup system for
the planet's plant resources.

Built to stand the test of time, this state-of-the-art vault can
withstand any disaster from bombings to earthquakes, and it is the
product of a partnership between The Global Crop Diversity Trust
and the Consultative Group on International Agricultural Research
(CGIAR). They collected seeds from seed banks all over the world to
be stored in the underground vault.

The seeds in the vault are stored under "black box" arrangements,
meaning the boxes will never be opened by anyone except the
original depositor, somewhat like a bank depository box. The
location means that even if there is a power outage or blackout,
the seed samples will remain frozen under the thick rock and
permafrost. The vault is considered the ultimate insurance policy for
the world's food supply.

THE VAVILOV INSTITUTE
OF PLANT INDUSTRY RUSSIA

Established by Nikolai Vavilov in the 1920s in Leningrad, this is
the oldest seed bank in the world and the only facility of its kind
in Russia. Its global collection contains hundreds of thousands of
specimens (see page 34).

NAVDANYA INDIA

Founded by Dr. Vandana Shiva, physicist, philosopher,
and renowned environmental activist, Navdanya protects
biodiversity and provides direction and support to
environmental activism and small farmers. It has its own
seed bank and organic farm spread over 20 acres (8 ha)
in Uttrakhand, India, and has successfully conserved more
than 5,000 crop cultivars and established 65 community
seed banks in 16 states across India (see page 16).
www.navdanya.org

BELOW A conservationist
examines seeds in the cold
storage vault at Kew's
Millennium Seed Bank.

KEW'S MILLENNIUM SEED BANK

The Millennium Seed Bank Partnership is the largest *ex situ* plant conservation project in the world. Its aim is to save seeds from plants all over the world, focusing on those most endangered and with the greatest potential future use. It has partners in more than fifty countries worldwide: Australia, Botswana, China, Mexico, Kenya, and Madagascar are just a few. Together they have saved more than 10 percent of the world's wild plant species and have banked over a billion seeds from about 130 different countries. Unfortunately, many plants become extinct before they can be collected, but in the bank there are a number of species now saved that have become extinct in the wild.

Each seed collection is "backed up" in a seed bank in the country of origin. The facilities are extensive from liquid nitrogen to a seed X-ray machine, but a lot of the work is done by hand with sieves and tweezers and the help of hardworking staff and volunteers.

Kew's scientists travel to many countries, specifically targeting regions where plants are at risk from climate change and the increasing impact of human activities. By 2020, they aim to secure the safe storage of seeds from 25 percent of the world's plants.

WHY KEW SAVES SEEDS

Scientific studies show that humans have changed ecosystems more widely and rapidly in the past fifty years than in any other comparable historical period, and today about one-fifth of all plant species face extinction. Concern for the earth's flora, in the face of such threats, drives Kew's mission to inspire and deliver science-based plant conservation worldwide.

HOW YOU CAN SUPPORT THE MSB

You and your community can support Kew's campaign in a number of ways. You can join in its annual seed swap, make a donation toward its research, or "adopt a seed" to help save a species. www.kew.org

ABOVE A scientist at Kew tests out different germination techniques.

Tip

Kew offer informative literature on seed saving, including some wonderful seed-saving tips. See its Web site for details www.kew.org

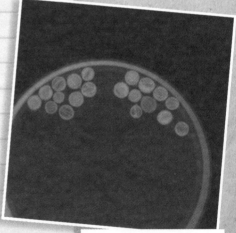

ABOVE X-rayed seeds from Kew's Millennium Seed Bank.

CREATE A
SEED BANK

GETTING STARTED

From the moment you put a seed into the ground, seeds of thought should be sown in your mind: How will I gather and save the seeds from this plant, what do I need for this process, and where will I store the seeds so they will last for many years to come?

GATHERING AND STORING

Seeds are part of a plant's life cycle, and saving them should be given as much thought as all the other stages of plant growth.

WHAT YOU NEED: Pruners, loppers, scissors, gloves, labels, a pen, a pillowcase/cloth bag, paper bags, and a bucket, basket, or bowl.

GATHERING SEEDS

The type of harvesting method chosen largely depends on the natural dispersal of the plant. For example, wind-dispersed seeds can simply be shaken out of their seed pods, but if these are from a tree, you may need long-handle pruners to reach them. Dry seeds can be harvested into a paper bag or pillowcase, as opposed to wet seeds, such as tomatoes, where a bucket makes a better receptacle.

CONTAINERS TO STORE

Professor César Gómez-Campo, of the Technical University of Madrid, tested forty different types of containers for their ability to exclude water vapor. Only sealed brass cans, canning jars with rubber seals, laboratory bottles with a screw cap and polyethlene seal (normally used for liquid chemicals), and flame-sealed glass ampoules prevented the intake of moisture sufficiently for long-term seed storage. Plastic, glass, metal, or foil containers let moisture in after two or three years and were good for only short-term storage.

Tip

Try to avoid collecting seeds or fruit that has been lying on the ground, because they may have experienced insect attack or have aged.

Tip

Old camera film canisters make good containers for storing small amounts of seeds, and these can then be put in canning jars to double the protection.

DO-IT-YOURSELF SEED BANK

Follow the checklist below and establish your own community seed bank.

1. Harvest your seeds from healthy plants, and remember to keep labels on your collection at all stages.

2. Keep seeds clean and dry indoors—remember seeds are alive and careful treatment will keep them alive for longer.

3. Store and label in airtight containers.

4. Dedicate a cool, dry, dark place for your collection—the refrigerator is perfect.

5. Invest in a dedicated refrigerator if you are a serious saver.

6. Add desiccants if you open your saved seed jars regularly, because your seeds will be exposed to moisture and desiccants can be used to keep them dry (see page 41).

7. Keep some seeds for swapping, which will help to increase the diversity of your collection.

ABOVE You can purchase equipment to start your own seed bank. This kit is available from Kew Gardens.

MAKING THE MOST OF A SEED SWAP

Before you attend a seed swap, you might want to write a wish list. There may be some rare and beautiful species that everyone wants, and in that case you might want to bring along any rare and beautiful species that you own to use as a bartering tool. Remember to only exchange for seeds that will suit your garden, location, soil, and size of plot, and try not to take home more than you can grow, because the seeds might go unused and someone else at the swap might appreciate them.

BE PREPARED

Take a camera, notebook, and pen to record interesting tips and hints as well as for taking notes at talks and workshops. There's always plenty of information, leaflets, and business cards to take home, and this is something you might want to provide for your exchanges, too. Most of all, enjoy yourself.

ABOVE Seed swaps, such as the Great Seed Swap at Wakehurst Place in England, are a great way to source new seeds.

"One person's seed is another person's garden."

JOSIE JEFFERY

ORGANIZING AND LABELING

Hordes of enthusiasts attend seed swaps, and they can get busy! If you plan to host or attend a meeting, organize how you will display your seeds ahead of time, and make your own seed envelopes decorated with hand-drawn illustrations or with printed images. Include all relevant information on the label, including the plant name, date and location of harvest, and any growing tips. Add 1 to 2 teaspoons of seeds per packet.

If you are having a stand at a seed swap, keep your seeds in categorized boxes so people can navigate through them easily. See it as a portable seed library; they could be organized alphabetically or by habit.

ABOVE AND BELOW Label all seed packets clearly, with the seed name, date, and growing tips. You can use this template to make your own seed envelopes.

ENVELOPE TEMPLATE

TOP FLAP

BACK FLAP
(covers bottom and side flaps)

FRONT

SIDE FLAP

BOTTOM FLAP

RAISING SEEDS

MEDIUM AND CONTAINERS

Before you sow your seeds, you need to have the right growing medium, additives, and containers.

GROWING MEDIUM

Use a peat-free seed-starting mix, which is ecofriendly and finer than a normal soil mix. It makes better contact with the seeds. A seed-starting mix also contains fewer nutrients, because they are not necessary for germinating seedlings, which use the food supply stored in the seeds. Potting mix can be used for transplanting. To help with drainage, aeration, and water retention, add one part horticultural water-retaining granules to two parts soil mix.

CONTAINERS

Plastic trays Use these for small seeds. They are cheap, retain warmth, and are washable, reusable, and strong.

Wooden trays These are costly but will last for years if looked after. They retain warmth and the strong aroma of cedar wood can deter pests and diseases.

Seed flats and 3 inch (7.5 cm) pots Use these for large seeds that are sown individually or in twos or threes, such as corn or beans. This limits transplant shock.

Recycled containers Reuse plastic food containers, cans, buckets, and old boots, etc. First clean them and punch in drainage holes.

Accessories Clear plastic covers can be used to keep seedlings warm, and capillary matting is a synthetic fiber that is placed under containers to supply them with greater reserves of water.

ABOVE Be inventive with your containers; use an old boot or recycle a can.

SODA BOTTLE POTS

Recycle a plastic bottle to make a self-watering pot by cutting it in half. Punch drainage holes with a hot needle in the "spout" end and remove the lid. Place the top end of the bottle, upside down, into the bottom half, making sure the spout touches the bottom. Fill the top end with seed-starting mix, packing it firmly into the spout. Sow seeds and water. The water will collect in the bottle bottom, which acts as a reservoir, and will be drawn up through the spout by capillary action.

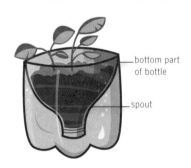

SODA BOTTLE POTS

bottom part of bottle

spout

ABOVE Cells in a plastic seed flat are ideal for larger seeds, such as corn and beans.

SEED-SOWING TECHNIQUES

Seeds can be sown indoors or directly outdoors, depending on the type of plant and the time of year. Note that some seeds need specific sowing treatments, such as scarification, stratification, or light exclusion before they will germinate. Make sure you do your research before you sow.

SOWING INDOORS

Fill the container with seed-starting mix, level, firm gently, and then water well.

For dustlike seeds, such as foxgloves, mix the seeds with fine, dry sand before sowing in shallow seed furrows to aid even distribution.

For small seeds, such as cornflowers, thinly sow on the soil mix surface and sift a thin layer of soil mix over them.

For large seeds, such as pumpkins, sow in seed-starting flats or 3 inch (7.5 cm) pots. Use two seeds pressed ¾ inch (2 cm) deep and ¾ inch (2 cm) apart per cell or pot.

Label the container with the name of the plant sown and the date. Use an ice-cream stick, or equivalent, as a label, and write using a permanent marking pen or pencil. Water the seeds lightly and cover the container with clear plastic, a sheet of glass or plastic wrap, or soda bottle greenhouses for pots (see page 60). Place somewhere warm and well lit, and check the seeds regularly. Keep the soil mix moist and transplant the seedlings when the first set of true leaves develop. It may be necessary to turn the container occasionally if the seedlings grow unevenly toward the light.

SOW DIRECTLY

Prepare the soil a few weeks before sowing by breaking up any clumps and removing rocks and weeds. Dig or rake in any soil improvers and level the surface. Weeding will need to be done again just before sowing, and the soil will also need to be raked once more to create a fine, crumblike texture on the surface. You can then broadcast, or scatter, your seeds and rake them in. Alternatively, you can sow seeds in rows, which are called seed furrows.

Mark where your seeds are, so you don't accidentally pull them up when you weed. It helps to research what your seedlings will look like. Water well with a fine spray.

Tip

Directly sown seeds may need protection, such as netting, from hungry wildlife.

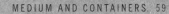

TOP DRESSINGS AND COVERINGS

Top dressing is where something is spread onto the surface of the soil, without it being dug in. In relation to seed growing, it usually applies to a layer of sand, fine grit, or vermiculite. Top dressing isn't a necessity, but it is a good technique for seed sowing because it helps retain moisture and prevent nutrients from leaching out. It also stops smaller seeds from washing away when you water your pots or flats. The thickness of the dressing varies according to seed type, but the larger the seed, the thicker the dressing can be.

GREENHOUSE EFFECT

To hold in heat and moisture, simply lay a sheet of plastic over the container or place it in a plastic bag. Remove the covering as soon as the seedlings emerge.

SODA BOTTLE GREENHOUSE

Plastic bottles, cut in half, can have much the same effect, and are often used outside to protect developing seedlings from pests and cold weather in spring. Use the top half of the bottle with the lid removed, and push it 2 inches (5 cm) into the soil over single plants.

COVERINGS

Seedlings and tender plants can be protected with tunnels made with pipes or wire bent into semicircles, then covered with floating row cover or clear plastic. Push the ends of the wire or pipes into the soil for stability. Store-bought tunnels are readily available online or in garden centers.

ABOVE This "Soda Bottle Greenhouse" provides early protection from pest predators and warmth to aid growth for young plants.

LEFT AND RIGHT Bendable plastic pipe can be used as a frame to cover your young plants with a floating row cover or plastic and later to cover with netting to keep pests off your crops.

WATERING SYSTEMS

After sowing seeds, the soil needs to be watered daily in order for seeds to germinate. The seeds need to take on water and swell, breaking the seed coat so they can emerge. A steady water supply will also be needed for the developing seedlings. In both cases, keep the soil moist but not so wet that it becomes waterlogged.

WATERING SEEDLINGS

Irrigate little and often because overwatering can cause diseases, such as damping-off. When watering, use a watering can with a rose for a fine spray, or a mist sprayer, to avoid disturbing the soil surface.

SODA BOTTLE DRIP IRRIGATION SYSTEM

When your plants have been planted, the rain will be their irrigation, but if there is prolonged dry weather you need to water, too. These soda bottle drip irrigation systems are perfect. Drip irrigation slowly delivers water into the soil directly around the roots. Watering spikes can be purchased from garden centers, but why not recycle and make your own for free?

1. Drill eight small holes into the cap of an empty plastic bottle.
2. Cut off the bottom of the bottle to create a funnel for filling and catching rainwater.
3. Bury the top third of the bottle by the plants, so that the spout is buried, and fill the bottle with water. Check the bottle daily and refill if needed. It can also be used for administering liquid fertilizer when necessary.

Tip

To save water and money, why not install a water barrel in your garden? You can harvest the rain from your gutters to irrigate your garden.

BELOW To save your plants from burning and to prevent unwanted evaporation, water them in the morning or late afternoon, when the sun is not as powerful.

DRIP IRRIGATION SYSTEM

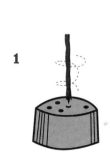
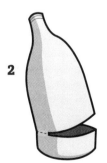

1 2 3

SEEDLINGS

Baby plants, known as seedlings, need a high level of care because they face many threats, such as mechanical damage, overwatering, drought, or pests and diseases. Seedlings have tender roots and shoots, and to make sure they survive, they must be handled gently until they are planted in the garden.

REPOTTING SEEDLINGS

Seedlings are usually repotted (moved to a larger pot) when the second set of leaves, known as "true leaves," develop. Overcrowded plants compete for space, water, and nutrients, so it will be necessary to thin out the weaker seedlings to let the stronger ones flourish.

1. Fill a seed-starting flat with potting mix and poke a hole in each cell with the blunt end of a pencil. Next, use the pointed end of the pencil to loosen the potting mix around one of the seedlings.

2. Hold the seedling by one of its seed leaves (the first set of leaves to appear), and gently pry the seedling out. It doesn't matter if you accidentally damage the leaf slightly, but if the roots break, the seedling will perish. Lower the roots into the hole that you made in the flat, and use the blunt end of the pencil to bed the seedling in.

3. Plant one seedling per cell to give it room to grow, then provide it with a fine spray of water, and label.

ABOVE These seedlings have developed their true leaves and are ready to be repotted individually into cells in a flat or larger pots.

REPOTTING SEEDLINGS

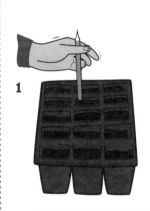
1

2

3

FEEDING AND MORE REPOTTING

A repotted seedling will need feeding every two weeks with a balanced liquid fertilizer, but check first, in case the potting mix you are using contains added fertilizer. Before you sow seeds straight into cells in a flat, you can mix slow-release fertilizer granules with the potting mix at the bottom of the cell to provide nutrients as their roots grow down into the potting mix.

REPOTTING LARGER PLANTS

Once the seedlings begin to outgrow their pots or cells, it will be necessary to move them into larger pots, unless they are already large enough to be planted directly into their final positions outdoors (see page 64).

1. To remove a plant from its cell or pot, turn it on its side and gently squeeze the sides and bottom to loosen the roots, allowing for it to fall out whole.

2. Put a thin layer of potting soil in the bottom of a 3 to 3½-inch (7 to 9 cm) pot and place the roots in whole.

3. Fill in with more potting soil and gently firm in, allowing a ½-inch (1 cm) gap between the top of the pot and the potting mix for watering. Label and water in.

ABOVE These celeriac seedlings will soon be ready to plant outdoors.

REPOTTING LARGER PLANTS

1

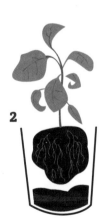

2

3

YOUNG PLANTS

Your indoor sown seedlings have grown from babies into juvenile plants. Like all juveniles, they need guidance and a helping hand to prepare them for "leaving the nest" or, in this case, uprooting from the warmth of a heated greenhouse into the garden where they will have to, for the most part, fend for themselves.

PLANTING OUTDOORS

The plants will still need some protection from potential threats ahead of them, and they will need to be hardened off.

HARDENING OFF

Your pampered indoor plants need to adjust to outdoor conditions prior to planting outdoors. One to two weeks in a cold greenhouse or a cold frame toughens them up by thickening the cuticle on the leaves and stems, making them stronger and more drought tolerant.

TRANSPLANTING

1. Water the plant the day before you transplant, and once again before you remove it from its pot.
2. Dig a hole slightly bigger than the roots, and water the hole before you add the plant.
3. Place the roots in the hole and fill halfway with water. Let the water settle around the roots. Fill the hole and lightly firm in the soil around the plant. Water again, and then water daily for the first couple of weeks.

Tip

Add well-rotted vegetable matter or garden compost to the planting hole for an extra boost, and top dress with a loose mulch, such as chipped bark.

TRANSPLANTING

CARING FOR PLANTS

Established plants still need care. Some may need support stakes and climbing trellises or trimming and pruning, and there is always weeding to be done. Regular weeding will stop weeds from competing with your plants for water and nutrients. The more weeds there are, the more your plants will struggle. Gardeners often remove old flowers, because this can promote additional flowering and sometimes the old flowers ruin the display. This technique is called deadheading, but don't deadhead your seed-saving plants because the seeds will be developing. Check the plants for any pests, diseases, and nutrient deficiencies. Telltale signs are changes in foliage color, spotting and holes on the leaves, wilting, and even total collapse.

Healthy, strong-growing plants are much less prone to pests and diseases, and one way to keep them healthy is to make sure they are well fed. The three major nutrients most plants need to thrive are nitrogen (N), which promotes leaf growth; phosphorus (P), for the roots and shoots; and potassium (K), for flowers and fruits. You will see these elements listed on packages of fertilizer, usually in different balances depending on the purpose of the fertilizer. Look for the NPK ratio. Some fertilizers also contain trace elements, such as magnesium and iron. Fertilizers are either natural in origin (such as fish, blood, and bone products) or entirely synthetic. Natural fertilizers tend to be slower acting, and if you are a "natural" gardener, they will fit better with your gardening ethos.

Keep plants in the ground well supplied with nutrients by preparing the soil well before planting, by digging in well-rotted manure to boost its fertility, or by growing a green manure (or cover crop) on the patch before sowing, such as buckwheat (right) or clover.

ABOVE You don't want your precious plants to have to compete with weeds, so weed regularly!

ABOVE This thriving vegetable patch is full of life and will produce an abundance of edible vegetables, and eventually, seeds that can be harvested.

MATURE PLANTS

Your plants have worked really hard so far and are now on their last push to complete their growing cycle. The flowers are about to bloom (a moment eagerly awaited by all), and this is the time to decide what steps to take to save "true" seeds.

LETTING IT GO TO SEED

Mark off some healthy plants for isolation. You should preferably choose plants that are in close proximity to each other, especially if you are building a cage around them. However, if you are bagging self-pollinating flowers, proximity isn't necessary. Your "true seed plants" will need monitoring, and you will find specific requirements under the entries in the Seed Directory.

Let the remaining plants in your garden accept the full flurry of hungry insects, bees, and butterflies. These pollinators will be hard at work, and the fruit and seeds that result will, in turn, give food to a whole other layer of garden wildlife, as well as produce for your kitchen table.

Your plants have completed their life cycle, from seed to flower and back to seed, and you have helped them every step of the way. Feel proud.

LEFT From seed to flower to seed—the circle is complete.

SEED DIRECTORY

INTRODUCTION

This seed directory consists of a collection of popular vegetables, such as pumpkin and eggplant, vegetables for salads, such as tomato, cucumber, and lettuce, along with herbs, such as cilantro and fennel, which are all complemented by decorative and useful flowers, such as hollyhock. There are also some more unusual plants featured here, such as okra and quinoa. The directory is split into sections covering vegetables, herbs, vegetables for salads, and flowers. Each profile has information on seed sowing, repotting, planting outdoors, and growing on to seed harvesting, processing, and seed-saving techniques. Each entry also includes an "ease" category, indicating how easy it is to grow and save seeds from that plant.

"Growing a garden is rewarding in so many ways. Plants just keep on giving, whether it is the gift of food, the gift of color and scent, or the gift of their offspring. Collecting and saving seeds, for me, is one of the most enjoyable gardening tasks."

JOSIE JEFFERY

Vegetables

Growing vegetables is one of the most satisfactory jobs for a gardener. The process of bringing food to the plate that you have grown on your vegetable patch is extremely rewarding and healthy for you and your pocket.

This section includes some of the most commonly grown and eaten vegetables, plus a few unusual ones.

"The greatest service which can be rendered to any country is to add a useful plant to its culture."

THOMAS JEFFERSON

EGGPLANT

Solanum melongena

WET SEED

DESCRIPTION: Native to India, the eggplant is a member of the Solanaceae family, whose members also include chilies and tomatoes. Eggplants are used worldwide in a variety of dishes, such as ratatouille, dips, and moussaka.

The eggplant is a 3-feet (1-m)-tall perennial with a prickly stem and large, coarse leaves. Its purple hermaphrodite flowers are followed by shiny, purple eggplants. Wild eggplants are yellow, bitter, and range from the size of a pea to the size of a baseball.

Eggplants cross-pollinate, so for seed saving, grow only one cultivar in isolation to be sure of purity. The flowers are self- and insect-pollinated.

SOW SEEDS: Sow indoors from 8 to 10 weeks before the last expected frost date in spring. Use a 3-inch (7.5 cm) pot and sow two seeds on the surface of the seed-starting mix. Cover with plastic wrap and place on a well-lit windowsill.

GERMINATION: 7 to 14 days

PLANT CARE: When the soil temperature reaches 60°F (15°C), grow in moist, well-drained soil, pH 5.8 to 6.8. Choose a warm and sunny, sheltered spot; stake for support. Leave 2 to 2½ feet (60 to 75 cm) between plants or grow individually in pots. In cool climates, grow eggplants in an unheated greenhouse so they will ripen. Water regularly and give a balanced liquid fertilizer once a month.

PESTS AND DISEASES: Flea beetles, red spider mites, Colorado potato beetles; fusarium wilt

YIELD: Four eggplants per plant, at least 12 weeks after sowing

HARVEST SEEDS: The seeds need to go through a process that mimics the natural fruit-rotting process; this can be done by storing overripe eggplants at room temperature for several weeks before seed harvesting. Scoop the seeds and pulp into a bowl of water and wring the pulp. Sieve, then dry on a labeled plate. Store in an airtight container.

For germinating next season, you may want to ferment half of the seeds (see page 46).

SPECIAL REQUIREMENTS: Caging • Isolation by 17 yards (16 m)

EASE: Moderate

SEED VIABILITY: 10+ years

BEET

Beta vulgaris

DESCRIPTION: This Mediterranean, biennial crop is famous for its deep purple roots. Its juice will stain everything it touches. Beet belongs to the Amaranthaceae family, whose members include spinach. The leaves and roots can be eaten raw or cooked.

The roots may be round, long, or oval in shape, and the skin color can range from yellow or white to dark red or purple. The baby leaves can be eaten raw, as a salad green.

For seed saving, wait for blooms in the second year of growth. The wind-pollinated flowers may cross-pollinate with other plants in the same family.

SOW SEEDS: Sow directly 2 to 3 weeks before the last expected frost date in spring, ¾-inch (2 cm) deep. Sow beets in succession every 3 weeks for a longer harvest. Overnight soaking before sowing will help soften the seed coat and speed germination.

GERMINATION: 7 to 30 days

PLANT CARE: Grow in a well-drained, weed-free, fertile soil, pH 6.0 to 6.8. Beet seeds are in clusters, so thin the seedlings as they emerge to a spacing of 2 to 4 inches (5 to 10 cm); the best way to do this is to cut the leaves off the surplus seedlings because this avoids damaging the developing roots of neighboring plants. Protect the remaining seedlings from predators by covering them with a cut plastic bottle. Keep the soil moist at all times, and in the second year, the flower heads may need support.

PESTS AND DISEASES: Aphids, carrot weevils, flea beetles, leaf miners, leafhoppers, and slugs; cerospora leaf spot

YIELD: One root per plant, about 55 days from sowing

HARVEST SEEDS: When the plant dies back after flowering, cut off the stem and hang it, upside down, in a paper bag. Once dry, strip the seed clusters off by hand. Store in an airtight container.

SPECIAL REQUIREMENTS: Caging • Isolation by 875 yards (800 m)

EASE: Labor intensive

SEED VIABILITY: 6 years

DRY SEED

CABBAGE
Brassica oleracea Capitata Group

DESCRIPTION: A Eurasian, biennial plant from the Brassicaceae family, whose members include broccoli, cauliflowers, turnips, and rutabaga. The plant is grown for its leaves, which have a great variety of culinary uses.

Cabbage plants are short, characterized by a dense, leafy cabbage "head" on a short stem. The leaves are usually green, but sometimes purple or with reddish tints. Cultivars are classified into spring, summer, fall, or winter types.

In the second year after planting, the plant sends up flowering shoots, goes to seed, and dies. The flowers are insect-pollinated and may cross-pollinate with other family members.

SOW SEEDS: Sow directly in ½-inch (1 cm) deep rows 6 inches (15 cm) apart. In cool climates, sow in spring for a summer and fall crop. In warmer areas (Zones 6 to 7), sow in early spring and harvest before the peak of summer, or sow in late summer for a fall crop. Sow in late winter for a spring harvest and late summer for a fall crop in Zones 8 and warmer; in some warm areas, cabbage can overwinter.

GERMINATION: 5 to 7 days

PLANT CARE: Choose a sunny or partly shaded site, with firm and fertile, free-draining soil, pH 6.5 to 7.5. Cabbage plants prefer cool weather and need a period of cold before they will flower and produce seed. Space plants 6 to 18 inches (15 to 45 cm) apart.

PESTS AND DISEASES: Aphids, caterpillars, cabbage loopers, flea beetles, cabbageworms; clubroot, fusarium wilt, downy mildew

YIELD: One head per plant, 10 to 36 weeks after sowing

HARVEST SEEDS: Keep at least six healthy plants for seed. When the seed pods turn brown, the seeds will scatter. Collect the seeds before this happens, so check daily. When the pods are dry, cut the entire plant down and lay on a sheet indoors to dry. Release the seeds by placing them in between two sheets and lightly trampling them with your feet. Dry thoroughly and store in an airtight container.

SPECIAL REQUIREMENTS: Caging
• Isolation by 1 mile (1.6 km) • Rice dry (see page 41)

EASE: Labor intensive

SEED VIABILITY: Up to 7 years

CARROTS
Daucus carota subsp. *sativus*

DRY SEED

DESCRIPTION: Carrots are biennial plants, native to Eurasia, and they belong to the Apiaceae family, along with close relatives fennel and celeriac. They are a popular root vegetable in most parts of the world, and their natural sweetness makes them popular in cakes and as a juice.

The attractive, ferny foliage is also edible, and the taproots that develop come in a variety of colors, including purple, red, white, and yellow, although the orange form is the most popular. If allowed to develop into the second year, white umbelliferous flower heads give rise to hundreds of tiny fruits called "mericarps." Each mericarp usually contains one seed.

Carrots are insect-pollinated and will cross-pollinate with wild carrot (*Daucus carota*).

SOW SEEDS: Sow directly 2 weeks before the last expected frost, ½ inch (1 cm) apart in rows ¾ inch (2 cm) deep. Allow 6 inches (15 cm) between rows.

GERMINATION: 14 days

PLANT CARE: Grow in full sun in a stone-free soil, pH 6.5 to 7.5. Improve the soil well before planting with well-rotted organic matter. Heavy, stony, infertile soils will cause the carrot roots to fork. Thin to 4 inches (10 cm) between individual plants. Mulch the crop with a thick layer of straw if keeping the plants in the soil over winter.

PESTS AND DISEASES: Aphids, carrot rust flies, wireworms; blight, damping-off

YIELD: One root per plant, 3 to 4 months after sowing

HARVEST SEEDS: Overwinter several roots and let them flower next season. When the flower umbels have turned brown and dry, cut them off with pruners and put them in a paper bag for about a week. Some people are allergic to the dust released while processing carrot seeds, so wear a dust mask and lay newspaper out on a flat surface. Rub the umbels between your hands to separate the seeds. Store the seeds in an airtight container.

SPECIAL REQUIREMENTS: Caging
• Isolation by 875 yards (800 m)

EASE: Labor intensive

SEED VIABILITY: 3 years

CELERIAC
Apium graveolens var. *rapaceum*

DESCRIPTION: This Mediterranean biennial is in the Apiaceae family, whose members include fennel and carrot. Its knobby "root" at the bottom of its stem is eaten raw or cooked and has a shelf life of up to 6 months if stored correctly.

The plants grow up to 3 feet (1 m) tall with heads of toothed, divided leaves. The swollen stem develops during the first summer, and if overwintered, flat-topped, creamy flower heads appear in the second summer.

The flowers are insect-pollinated and will cross-pollinate readily.

SOW SEEDS: Indoors in early spring, lightly press the seeds down into a flat of seed-starting mix and water from below. It can help to soak the seeds overnight to break down the hard seed coat. Cover the seed flat with a perforated sheet of plastic wrap to assist germination. When the seedlings show their first "true" leaves, harden them off for a week in a cold frame or unheated greenhouse. Transplant into the garden in mid- to late spring, 8 inches (20 cm) apart and in rows 18 inches (45 cm) apart.

GERMINATION: 14 to 21 days

PLANT CARE: Grow in full or part sun in a moist, fertile soil, pH 6.6 to 7.0. Water regularly every 4 to 7 days in summer and provide a mulch to conserve moisture. Top dress with a nitrogen-rich fertilizer if the leaves begin to pale. Toward midsummer, pluck off the outer leaves and mound up soil around the root to keep tender. Harvest after the first frost to improve flavor. Apply a thick mulch of straw to overwinter for seed saving.

PESTS AND DISEASES: Carrot rust flies, celery leafminers; none

YIELD: One root per plant, 4 to 5 months after sowing

HARVEST SEEDS: Overwinter three plants for seed saving and let them flower the next year. Let the seeds turn brown and dry completely before harvesting. Rub onto newspaper, let dry completely, and store in an airtight container.

SPECIAL REQUIREMENTS: Caging • Isolation by 1 mile (1.6 km)

EASE: Labor intensive

SEED VIABILITY: 5 years

CHILI
Capsicum spp.

WET SEED

DESCRIPTION: Native to the Americas, these short-lived, frost-tender perennials are members of the Solanaceae (tomato) family and produce hot chilies that change color as they ripen. The spiciness, shape, and size of the chilies are equally as varied.

Chilies make short, shrubby plants, with a plentiful supply of small, off-white flowers in the warmer months. Once pollinated, these soon develop into the edible "fruits."

The flowers are both self- and insect-pollinated, and they will readily cross-pollinate with other capsicums.

SOW SEEDS: In late winter, sterilize seed flats with boiling water and fill with seed-starting mix. Lightly cover the seeds with ¼ inch (5 mm) of seed-starting mix. Spray lightly with water daily. Place in a well-lit position indoors at a temperature of 65 to 70°F (18 to 21°C); only move seedlings outside once the risk of frost passes.

GERMINATION: 4 to 6 weeks

PLANT CARE: Best grown in a greenhouse or tunnel: keep the temperature above 65°F (18°C) at all times. Use a light, well-drained soil, pH 6.0. Allow a distance of about 20 inches (50 cm) between plants, or grow individually in pots. Aid drainage by adding perlite or vermiculite to the soil mix. Feed weekly with a balanced liquid fertilizer when the plants are in flower. Chilies can be picked when green, or let ripen so they develop their full color, although letting them ripen will reduce the overall yield.

PESTS AND DISEASES: Aphids, flea beetles, cutworms, tomato hornworms; tobacco mosaic virus, bacterial leaf spot

YIELD: Many chilies per plant, 4 to 5 months after sowing

HARVEST SEEDS: Select healthy, unblemished, fully ripe fruits. Cut them open and extract the seeds. Place the seeds onto a kitchen towel until they are dry and brittle. Store in an airtight container using the rice dry method (see page 41), and place in the freezer. When handling chilies, wear gloves.

SPECIAL REQUIREMENTS: Bagging • Caging • Isolation by 165 feet (150 m)

EASE: Moderate

SEED VIABILITY: 5 years, or 10 years+ if frozen

ZUCCHINI
Cucurbita pepo

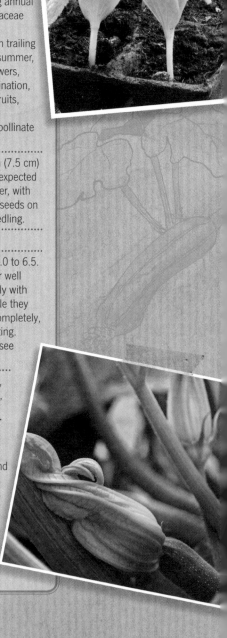

WET SEED

DESCRIPTION: Zucchini are low-growing, scrambling annual plants native to the Americas. They belong to the Curcubitaceae family along with pumpkins, and are eaten cooked or raw.

When in full growth, zucchini hold large, coarse leaves on trailing stems. Their yellow tubular flowers are borne mid- to late summer, starting with the male flowers, then later by the female flowers, which have an immature zucchini at the bottom. After pollination, these develop into shiny green to white, long to rounded fruits, often with stripes or mottled spots.

The flowers are insect-pollinated, and they readily cross-pollinate with other closely related plants.

SOW SEEDS: Indoors, sow seeds individually in 3-inch (7.5 cm) pots at a depth of 1 inch (2.5 cm) 2 weeks before the last expected frost. In warm areas, sow the seeds directly in early summer, with two seeds together at a depth of 1 inch (2.5 cm). Sow the seeds on their side. If both seeds germinate, remove the weaker seedling.

GERMINATION: 7 days

PLANT CARE: Grow on well-drained, fertile soil, pH 6.0 to 6.5. Mulch and feed with a general-purpose fertilizer, and water well throughout the growing season. Once in flower, feed weekly with a balanced liquid fertilizer. For eating, harvest zucchini while they are small and tender. For seeds, let the zucchini enlarge completely, resting them on a piece of stone to prevent them from rotting. To produce "true" seeds, you may want to hand-pollinate (see page 27).

PESTS AND DISEASES: Aphids, cucumber beetles, leafhoppers, sqash bugs, squash vine borers; mosaic virus, powdery mildew

YIELD: Sixteen per plant, 2 to 3 months after sowing

HARVEST SEEDS: Harvest about 20 days after the zucchini matures. Pull out the pulp and seeds and wash and sieve. Dry on a labeled plate for a few weeks, then store in an airtight container.

SPECIAL REQUIREMENTS: Hand-pollination
- Isolation by 875 yards (800 m)

EASE: Moderate

SEED VIABILITY: 6 to 10 years

LEEK
Allium porrum

DRY SEED

DESCRIPTION: This Eurasian biennial plant is a member of the Alliaceae family, sitting alongside onions, shallots, and garlic. Instead of producing a bulb, it produces a long stem of edible bundled leaves. Leeks have many culinary purposes.

Unlike onions, which die back in winter, leeks are evergreen and winter-hardy, making them a good vegetable from fall to spring. The flower head develops in the second season, making the stems inedible as its hard shaft forms within the leaf bundle.

Leeks are insect-pollinated and will cross with other cultivars of leek. Note that they will not cross with onions.

SOW SEEDS: In the North, sow indoors 10 weeks before the last expected frost date. In mild areas, sow directly in spring, in rows 12 inches (30 cm) apart and ½ inch (1 cm) deep. Thin a month later leaving 6 inches (15 cm) between plants; the surplus plants can be replanted elsewhere in the garden. Mark each row with sticks to avoid possible weeding accidents.

GERMINATION: 14 days

PLANT CARE: Grow in a sunny, sheltered spot in well-drained, fertile soil, pH 6.0 to 6.5. Harvest leeks when large enough to use. Leeks are an ideal crop to transplant into bare patches and even mixed into a flower border. Improve the soil the winter before planting with plenty of well-rotted organic matter. Feed with a general-purpose fertilizer and irrigate regularly.

PESTS AND DISEASES: Leek moths; leek rust

YIELD: One stem per plant, 5 to 6 months after sowing

HARVEST SEEDS: The seed head rests on a stem up to 6 feet (1.8 m) tall. They take longer than onions to ripen, and as they dry, they shatter and release the seeds; the trick is to get there before this happens. When you can see the seeds blacken within the drying flowers, cut the stem off and place, upside down, in a pillowcase, and leave it indoors for 3 weeks. Winnow and sieve the seeds gently. When dry, store in an airtight container.

SPECIAL REQUIREMENTS: Bagging
• Caging • Isolation by 1 mile (1.6 km)

EASE: Labor intensive

SEED VIABILITY: 3 to 9 years

OKRA
Abelmoschus esculentus

DRY SEED

DESCRIPTION: This 6-feet 6-inch (2 m) tall African plant belongs in the Malvaceae family along with hollyhock and hibiscus. It is an annual vegetable, prized for its pods. These pods exude a sticky goo when cut, which can be used to thicken soups.

Okra has large, lobed leaves and flowers that have five white to yellow petals with a red or purple dot at their bases. Each flower only blooms for a day and is followed by a hairy pod.

The flowers are self- and insect-pollinated.

SOW SEEDS: Okra seeds are big and easy to handle. Sow directly 2 weeks after the last frost at a depth of 1¼ inches (3 cm) and 4 to 8 inches (10 to 20 cm) apart, spacing the rows 4 inches (10 cm) apart. For an earlier start, sow seeds indoors 6 to 8 weeks before the transplant date; starting in pots will lessen the seedling transplant shock. Scarify or soak your seeds overnight to speed up germination.

GERMINATION: 6 days

PLANT CARE: Because okra thrives in hot and sunny, humid conditions, growing in a greenhouse may be required in cooler climates. Choose a sunny site in fertile, well-drained soil, pH 6.0 to 8.0, although poor soil is tolerated. Water well every 7 to 10 days and feed regularly with a high-nitrogen fertilizer. Space plants 15 to 24 inches (40 to 60 cm) apart; overcrowding will result in thin plants with few pods. Harvest the seed pods for eating when immature. If they reach a length of more than 4 inches (10 cm), they become fibrous and woody.

PESTS AND DISEASES: Root-knot nematodes; blight, fusarium wilt

YIELD: Numerous pods depending on the climate, 4 to 5 months after sowing

HARVEST SEEDS: The fruit capsule contains many seeds. It is best to leave the pod to mature and dry on the plant until it has browned. To release the seeds, twist and pull the pod apart over a bowl. Let dry thoroughly and store in an airtight container.

SPECIAL REQUIREMENTS: Caging • Isolation by 1 mile (1.6 km) • Skin irritant; wear gloves

EASE: Easy

SEED VIABILITY: 4 years

ONION
Allium cepa

DESCRIPTION: Native to Eurasia, onions belong to the Alliaceae family along with leeks and chives. Onions are biennial plants, widely cultivated for their flavorful bulbs with yellow, white, red, or brown papery skins.

Onions are short plants, bearing narrow leaves that mature in the first summer as the bulb swells. The leaves die down in winter, and in the second season, the plants will flower and set seed.

The round flower heads are insect-pollinated, and crossbreeding can occur between varieties.

SOW SEEDS: Sow seed indoors in a seed flat 8 to 12 weeks before planting outdoors. Sow seeds in moistened seed-starting mix, and on germination, harden off the seedlings in a cold frame before planting outside 4 to 6 inches (10 to 15 cm) apart in spring. Or sow the seeds directly where they are to grow in spring. In warm areas, make a second sowing of short-day cultivars in fall or winter. Sow seeds sparingly to keep thinning out to a minimum.

GERMINATION: 14 days

PLANT CARE: Grow in sunny, well-drained, fertile soil, pH 6.0 to 7.0. Prepare with well-rotted manure 6 months before planting. Weed regularly but be careful not to damage the bulbs. Water regularly once the plants are established. Harvest the bulbs in late summer and hang them to dry before storing. To collect the seeds, let plants overwinter and then flower; groups of plants can be bagged and hand-pollinated every day for 2 weeks.

PESTS AND DISEASES: Onion flies, onion root maggots, thrips, wireworms; downy mildew, damping-off

YIELD: One bulb per plant, 4 to 6 months after sowing

HARVEST SEEDS: Let seeds mature and dry on the plants, then cut the whole stem and place the seed head into a pillowcase. Hang up the pillowcase indoors and dry for 3 weeks. Winnow and sieve the seeds, dry thoroughly, then store in an airtight container.

SPECIAL REQUIREMENTS: Caging
• Isolation by 1 mile (1.6 km)

EASE: Labor intensive

SEED VIABILITY: 2 years

PARSNIP
Pastinaca sativa

DRY SEED

DESCRIPTION: A biennial root crop native to Eurasia, the parsnip belongs to the Apiaceae family along with carrot and celery. Parsnips are grown for their flavorful, conical white roots, which are best eaten cooked and are delicious when roasted.

The leaves are divided like celery and strongly scented. Parsnip grows up to 6 feet 6 inches (2 m) in height, and the tall stems produce flat heads of little yellow flowers in the second year, followed by papery seeds.

The flowers are pollinated by insects and will readily cross-pollinate with closely related garden weeds.

SOW SEEDS: Sow seeds where they are to grow in spring. Sow in groups of three about ½ inch (15 mm) deep and in rows 18 inches (45 cm) apart. In warm areas, sow in late fall for a spring crop.

GERMINATION: Up to 21 days

PLANT CARE: Best in a loose, deep, freely draining, sandy soil, pH 6.5. Choose a sunny site and enrich the soil with well-rotted manure a few months before sowing. Keep the site free from weeds and make sure that the soil is reliably moist in dry weather. Frost improves and sweetens their flavor, so harvest the roots after a frost. For seed saving, choose about ten of the healthiest-looking plants and overwinter with a thick mulch of straw; in the second year, the flower stems may need support. Discard any plants that start to flower long before the others because there is a risk of developing a strain that bolts.

PESTS AND DISEASES: Root-knot nematodes, carrot rust flies, onion maggots; parsnip canker

YIELD: One root per plant, 5 months after sowing

HARVEST SEEDS: Let the flowers mature on the plant in late summer. When they brown, remove the stem and place it, upside down, in a pillowcase. Let dry indoors for a few weeks, then winnow the seeds and store in an airtight container.

SPECIAL REQUIREMENTS: Caging • Isolation by 875 yards (800 m) • Skin irritant; wear gloves

EASE: Moderate

SEED VIABILITY: 1 year

PEAS
Pisum sativum

DESCRIPTION: An annual climbing plant native to Asia and Africa, peas belong to the Leguminosae family along with beans and clover. Peas are grown for their sweet edible pods and seeds (peas).

Peas are scrambling plants, varying in height from 12 inches to 6 feet (30 cm to 1.8 m) tall, depending on the cultivar. Pea cultivars are divided into three groups: shelling, snap, and snow peas. The pods of snap and snow peas are eaten whole, without shelling. Shelling peas have different maturity times: early, mid-season, and late.

Peas are self-pollinating and do not readily cross, but to be sure of purity follow the methods detailed under special requirements.

SOW SEEDS: Peas do best in temperatures of 50 to 70°F (10 to 21°C). Sow seeds directly where they are to grow in early spring or late summer; in warm areas, grow as a winter crop. Sow seeds 1 inch (2.5 cm) deep and 3 to 4 inches (7.5 to 10 cm) apart.

GERMINATION: 14 days

PLANT CARE: Grow in a nutrient-rich, moisture-retentive soil, pH 5.8 to 7.0. Keep the site free of weeds, and provide support as they grow. Water well once the plants start to flower to build the crop. For seed saving, pick ten healthy plants and pull up any plants that look weak or have distorted or mottled leaves.

PESTS AND DISEASES: Aphids, pea weevils, slugs; powdery mildew, root rot, fusarium wilt

YIELD: About 2 pounds (1 kg) per 3-foot (1-m) row, 3 to 4 months after sowing

HARVEST SEEDS: Because there is a risk of rain inducing mold while the seeds are drying, it may be best to harvest plants whole and hang them up indoors on a laundry line. When the pods are completely dry, they can be threshed in between two sheets of paper or cloth. They will crumble and release the seeds easily. Store in an airtight container.

SPECIAL REQUIREMENTS: Bagging • Caging • Isolation by 50 feet (15 m)

EASE: Easy

SEED VIABILITY: 2 years

PUMPKIN

Cucurbita spp.

WET SEED

DESCRIPTION: A low and scrambling North American annual plant from the Curcubitaceae family, the pumpkin is a close relative of the zucchini and cucumber. These plants vary in size, shape, and color. The flesh and the seeds are used to make soups and breads.

Pumpkins have large, coarse leaves and large, yellow tubular flowers, that are borne in mid- to late summer, starting with the male flowers, and soon followed by the female flowers, which are easily identified because they have an immature fruit at the bottom. On pollination, these soon begin to swell.

Pumpkin flowers are insect-pollinated, and they readily cross-pollinate with other closely related plants. Plants grown under cover may need to be hand-pollinated to be sure of pumpkins.

SOW SEEDS: Indoors, sow in 3-inch (7.5 cm) pots 3 weeks before the last expected spring frost. Place a seed in on its side at a depth of 1 inch (2.5 cm) and cover. Or sow seeds directly when the soil temperature reaches 60°F (15.5°C).

GERMINATION: 7 days

PLANT CARE: Grow on well-drained, fertile soil, pH 6.0 to 6.5. Mulch and feed with a general-purpose fertilizer, and water well throughout the growing season. Once in flower, feed weekly with a balanced liquid fertilizer. For eating, harvest while small and tender. For seeds, let the pumpkins enlarge completely. To hand-pollinate, rub the stamen of a male flower onto the stigma of a female flower.

PESTS AND DISEASES: Gray squash bugs, squash vine borers, cucumber beetles; mosaic virus, powdery mildew, bacterial wilt, anthracnose

YIELD: One to ten pumpkins per plant, depending on cultivar, 4 to 5 months after sowing

HARVEST SEEDS: Let the fruit mature until the skin cannot be dented with a fingernail. Keep indoors to mature for 3 weeks, then scoop out the pulp and seeds. Wash, separating the seeds from the pulp, then dry the seeds on a labeled plate for a few weeks. Store in an airtight container.

SPECIAL REQUIREMENTS: Hand-pollination
- Isolation by 875 yards (800 m)

EASE: Moderate

SEED VIABILITY: 4 to 9 years

RUNNER BEANS
Phaseolus coccineus

DESCRIPTION: Native to the Americas, and belonging to the Leguminosae family along with peas and peanuts, runner beans are tall, climbing plants, but dwarf cultivars are available. The flowers appear just before midsummer. The seeds are strikingly mottled, particularly when fresh.

The red, white, or bicolored flowers are insect-pollinated and will cross-pollinate with other cultivars of runner bean. They will not cross with other species of bean.

SOW SEEDS: For direct sowing, sow when the soil temperature is at least 60°C (15.5°C). Space the seeds 6 inches (15 cm) apart, and sow two seeds together in case one fails to germinate. For an early start, sow seeds indoors with two seeds per pot, at a depth of 2 inches (5 cm). When the risk of frost has passed, harden the seedlings off and plant outdoors; they may need up to 10 days to get established after transplanting.

GERMINATION: 14 days

PLANT CARE: Yields are best in a sheltered site, in a rich, deeply cultivated, well-drained soil, pH 6.5 to 7.0. Runner beans can grow up to 10 feet (3 m), and need something to twist and climb on; an A-frame or tepee made of stakes and ties is the typical structure, with one stake per plant, set at 6 inches (15 cm) apart. Pinch off the growing tips once the plants reach the top of the support. Water regularly in dry weather, as the flower buds emerge.

PESTS AND DISEASES: Aphids, leaf miners, Mexican bean beetles, bean leaf beetles; anthracnose, root rot, blight

YIELD: About 1 pound (2 kg) per 3-foot (1-m) row, 2 to 3 months after sowing

HARVEST SEEDS: Let the pods dry and turn crispy on the plant for as long as possible into fall. Pod small quantities of beans by hand; thresh larger quantities in a pillowcase by placing it in a garbage can and shaking vigorously. Discard any beans that are discolored, shriveled, or have insect holes in them and store the good ones in an airtight container.

SPECIAL REQUIREMENTS: Bagging • Caging
• Isolation by 875 yards (800 m)

EASE: Moderate

SEED VIABILITY: 3 years

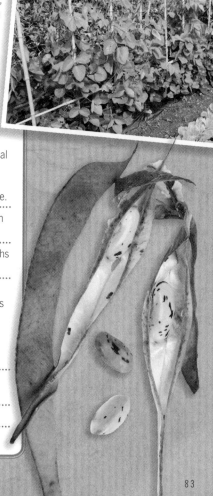

RUTABAGA

Brassica napus var. *napobrassica*

DESCRIPTION: A biennial winter vegetable native to Europe, rutabaga belongs to the Brassicaceae family, along with its relatives cabbage and cauliflower. It is grown for its sweet root with yellow or orange flesh and a leathery, dark purple skin. The root is used mashed and in wholesome soups, and the leaves can be eaten as a steamed green.

DRY SEED

Rutabagas are slow-growing, hardy vegetables that can overwinter in the ground, where they can be lifted as needed or left to grow into the second year when the plants will flower. The stalks bear many tiny, mustard-yellow flowers, which develop into seed pods. The plant has completed its life cycle after seeding.

The flowers are insect-pollinated, and rutabaga will cross-pollinate with any of its relatives in the Brassicaceae family.

SOW SEEDS: Sow seeds directly in early to midsummer for a fall harvest. Sow thinly ½ to ¾ inch (1 to 2 cm) deep in rows 15 inches (40 cm) apart. Thin out the seedlings in stages until the plants are 8 to 10 inches (20 to 25 cm) apart.

GERMINATION: 5 to 7 days

PLANT CARE: Grow in full sun or part shade, in firm and fertile, free-draining soil, pH 6.5 to 7.5. Prepare the soil with well-rotted manure some months before planting out. Rutabaga is easy to grow and has few demands other than to keep the weeds at bay, and watering when the weather is dry. Dress the plants with a general-purpose fertilizer before the root starts to swell. Overwinter up to six healthy plants if saving for seeds.

PESTS AND DISEASES: Army worms, flea beetles, cabbage root maggots, leafhoppers; clubroot

YIELD: One root per plant, 20 to 26 weeks after sowing

HARVEST SEEDS: Let the slender green seed pods develop and mature until brown on the plant, then cut the entire plant down and lay on a sheet indoors to dry. The seeds can be released by being trampled between sheets. Store in an airtight container.

SPECIAL REQUIREMENTS: Caging • Isolation by 1 mile (1.6 km) • Rice dry (see page 41)

EASE: Moderate

SEED VIABILITY: 2 years

SWEET CORN
Zea mays

DRY SEED

DESCRIPTION: Native to the Americas, sweet corn belongs to the Poaceae family, which means that it is a type of grass and is closely related to other grass crops, such as wheat and barley.

Corn is like no other vegetable, growing tall with long, strap-shape leaves and strange flowers and ears.

It has separate male and female flowers, both on the same plant. The male flowers, called tassels, sit on the top of the stalks, where they shed pollen. The wind carries the pollen to the "silk" that grows out of the corncobs, which emerge in the leaf axils. The flowers cross-pollinate with other corn cultivars.

SOW SEEDS: In cool climates, start indoors one week before the last expected spring frost. Sow one seed per cell in a seed flat, 1¼ to 1½ inches (3 to 4 cm) deep. Plant out only when the risk of frost has passed, into a block pattern, with the plants 18 inches (45 cm) apart. Or sow the seeds directly where they are to grow, at the same spacing, one week after the last expected spring frost. Sow two seeds together in case one fails to germinate; remove the weakest of each pair when ¾ inch (2 cm) tall.

GERMINATION: 10 days

PLANT CARE: Choose a sheltered, sunny spot in moist but well-drained soil, pH 5.8 to 6.5. Protect seedlings with a floating row cover in cooler climates. Water and weed regularly. To provide stability, soil can be hilled up around the bottom of the stem.

PESTS AND DISEASES: Earworms, aphids, cucumber beetles, cutworms, flea beetles, Japanese beetles, thrips, wireworms; bacterial wilt, smut

YIELD: One to two cobs per plant, 4 to 5 months after sowing

HARVEST SEEDS: Remove the cobs from the plant 4 to 6 weeks after the eating stage, or wait until the husks turn brown. Pull back the husks and finish drying in a cool, dry place. To separate the seeds from the cobs, grip and twist the dried cobs, letting the kernels fall into a container. Winnow and then store in an airtight container.

SPECIAL REQUIREMENTS: Caging • Isolation by 1 mile (1.6 km)

EASE: Easy

SEED VIABILITY: 3 years

TURNIP

Brassica rapa subsp. *rapa*

DRY SEED

DESCRIPTION: This biennial, Eurasian winter vegetable belongs to the Brassicaceae family, whose members include cabbage and radish. It is most often grown for its tender, flavorsome root, which can be eaten raw or cooked, but the whole plant is edible. In the first year, all energy is diverted into developing the storage root. In the second year, the energy stored in the root fuels the formation of flowers and then the seeds.

The flowers are insect-pollinated and will cross readily with other *Brassica* plants.

SOW SEEDS: Directly sow seeds in spring about 1 month before the last expected spring frost. Sow thinly ½ to ¾ inch (1 to 2 cm) deep in rows 10 to 12 inches (25 to 30 cm) apart. Thin out the seedlings in stages until the plants are 8 to 10 inches (20 to 25 cm) apart if you are growing for roots, or to 6 inches (15 cm) apart if you are growing for turnip greens.

GERMINATION: 5 to 7 days

PLANT CARE: Grow in full sun or part shade, in firm and fertile, free-draining soil, pH 6.5 to 7.5. Prepare the soil with well-rotted manure some months before planting. Turnips are easy to grow and have few demands other than weeding, and watering regularly when the weather is dry to avoid woody or split roots. If the turnips are overwintered for seed saving, provide extra protection with a floating row cover or a thick mulch of straw. Retain up to six strong, healthy plants for seed saving.

PESTS AND DISEASES: Aphids, cabbage root maggots, flea beetles; clubroot

YIELD: One root per plant, 6 to 12 weeks after sowing

HARVEST SEEDS: Let the slim green seed pods develop and mature on the plant until they brown, then cut down the entire plant and lay on a sheet indoors to dry. Lay the seed heads between two sheets and trample to release the seeds. Winnow, let dry thoroughly, and store in an airtight container.

SPECIAL REQUIREMENTS: Caging • Isolation by 1 mile (1.6 km) • Rice dry (see page 41)

EASE: Moderate

SEED VIABILITY: 5 years

Herbs

Herbs are well respected plants and have been used since prehistoric times as both medicinal remedies and for flavoring food. They represent a huge, diverse group and can be found growing in most parts of the world, from the most difficult mountaintop conditions to shaded woodlands.

There are many benefits to growing your own herbs. For example, there's nothing like fresh lavender flowers in a hot bath or a salad garnished with basil plucked from the garden just a few minutes before. It is their hidden qualities that make herbs so valued: some have the ability to heal, others the power to soothe. Some are simply indispensable in the kitchen, and many are worth growing purely for their ornamental traits. Chamomile, for example, is a pretty garden herb with its daisy flowers, yet a tea made from its feathery leaves will calm and soothe a restless mind, promoting sleep.

BASIL
Ocimum basilicum

DRY SEED

DESCRIPTION: Basil is a perennial herb native to tropical parts of Asia, grown for its aromatic, sweet leaves, that are used in many dishes. A member of the Lamiaceae family, it is closely related to many other popular herbs, such as mint and thyme.

Basil has many cultivars, with a striking range of flavors, and the plants can grow up to 2 feet (60 cm) tall. In cool climates, the plants are usually treated as annuals. As well as the green leaves, the seeds and the white spires of flowers are edible. Basil is said to have anti-inflammatory and antioxidant properties that help circulation, stabilize blood sugar levels, and improve respiration.

The flowers are insect-pollinated, so only grow one variety to avoid cross-pollination.

SOW SEEDS: Sow seeds indoors 4 to 6 weeks before the last expected spring frost. Sow ten seeds in a 3-inch (7.5 cm) pot filled with damp seed-starting mix. Cover the seeds with a thin layer of mix, then stretch a piece of plastic wrap over the top of the pot. Place the pot on a warm, sunny windowsill, and when the seedlings emerge, remove the wrap. When the seedlings are 2 inches (5 cm) tall, repot into their own 3-inch (7.5 cm) pots, and return them to the windowsill. Transplant them outside only when the risk of frost has passed. Alternatively, sow directly outdoors when all danger of frost has passed and the soil temperature is at least 60°F (15.5°C).

GERMINATION: 5 days

PLANT CARE: Choose a warm, sheltered spot if you are growing it outside, in full sun, in a free-draining soil, pH 5.5 to 6.5. To promote bushy growth, harvest leaves frequently and pinch off the stem directly above a pair of leaves.

PESTS AND DISEASES: Slugs; fusarium wilt, damping-off

HARVEST SEEDS: Each capsule usually has four seeds. When they turn black, cut the spikes off and place indoors, in a pillowcase, to dry. Trample or rub out the seeds, then winnow, sieve, and store in an airtight container.

SPECIAL REQUIREMENTS: Bagging
• Caging • Isolation by 500 yards (450 m)

EASE: Easy

SEED VIABILITY: 5 years

BORAGE
Borago officinalis

DESCRIPTION: Borage is an annual herb from the Mediterranean region, belonging to the Boraginaceae family alongside forget-me-nots and comfrey. Its sky-blue, star-shaped flowers make decorative additions to salads, cakes, and drinks, and its large leaves have a cucumber aroma; they can be eaten raw or cooked. Herbal preparations of borage are said to soothe colds and digestive and skin problems. Consumption is not recommended during pregnancy or for people with liver or kidney complaints.

Borage can make a reasonably large, spreading plant up to 2 feet 4 inches (70 cm) tall. It bears plenty of star-shaped blue flowers in summer. The leaves are rough and prickly.

The flowers are capable of pollinating themselves, but are usually pollinated by insects. Plant borage with strawberries to improve strawberry yield and strengthen insect and disease resistance in nearby plants. Because bees love borage, it is a good plant where pollination is needed.

SOW SEEDS: A week before the last expected spring frost, sow seeds directly where they are to grow ¾ inch (2 cm) deep in rows 12 inches (30 cm) apart.

GERMINATION: 7 to 14 days

PLANT CARE: Borage grows easily in most soil, pH 4.3 to 8.5, providing there is adequate drainage. It can grow in full sun or semishade, and will even tolerate dry, infertile ground, but the plants appreciate being watered well. Top-heavy plants may need sticks for support.

PESTS AND DISEASES: Aphids; none

HARVEST SEEDS: After the flowers fade, they close up around the developing seeds and hang down. The sepals remain green even when the seeds are ripe. There are usually four seeds per flower; these are green when immature, and turn black when they are ripe and can be simply plucked. Dry the seeds indoors and store in an airtight container.

SPECIAL REQUIREMENTS: Caging
• Isolation by 875 yards (800 m)

EASE: Easy

SEED VIABILITY: 5 to 10+ years

CORIANDER (CILANTRO)

Coriandrum sativum

DRY SEED

DESCRIPTION: This aromatic, annual herb is native to Eurasia and belongs to the Apiaceae family, along with carrot and fennel. Its leaves, know as cilantro, are used in salads, curries, and soups, and the seeds are widely used as a culinary spice, either crushed, ground, or whole. Coriander is said to reduce flatulence and increase appetite, and a poultice made from the plant is believed to relieve rheumatism and painful joints.

Coriander makes a useful addition to the kitchen garden, where it can grow up to 20 inches (50 cm) tall. It bears flavorsome, feathery leaves and flat flower heads made up of many small white, or pinkish white, flowers. The flowers are pollinated by insects and will cross-pollinate with relatives; if this happens, the seeds produce inferior plants, often with an unpleasant flavor.

SOW SEEDS: Sow the seeds directly where they are to grow in spring after the danger of frost has passed, and in fall every 2 weeks for an ongoing supply. In cool areas, also sow in summer; in hot areas sow only from fall to early spring. Sow seeds directly into shallow rows 2 inches (5 cm) apart. Keep developing seedlings moist to prevent the plants from running to seed prematurely.

GERMINATION: 7 to 10 days

PLANT CARE: Grow in a light and fertile, well-drained soil, pH 6.5 to 7.5. For seed production, the plants are best in full sun; for better leaves, grow in part shade. Keep watering to a minimum. The leaves can be picked at any time.

PESTS AND DISEASES: None; none

HARVEST SEEDS: Harvest as soon as the seeds are brown, dry, and aromatic. The seeds fall readily from the seed head, so it is a good idea to cover bunches of about six heads together in a paper bag and hang them, upside down, in a warm, dry, and airy place. Alternatively, rub the heads together in your hands over a bucket, then place the gathered seeds on a tray of newspaper to dry. Winnow the chaff and store in an airtight container.

SPECIAL REQUIREMENTS: Bagging • Caging • Isolation by 875 yards (800 m)

EASE: Easy

SEED VIABILITY: 2 to 4 years

CHAMOMILE
Chamaemelum nobile

DRY SEED

DESCRIPTION: This aromatic meadow flower, native to Eurasia, belongs to the Asteraceae family along with sunflowers and marigolds. It is a hardy, perennial herb that forms a low covering of edible, bright green, feathery, sweetly scented leaves. The daisylike flower heads are also edible and bloom throughout summer.

The plants are best known for the tea that can be made from their feathery leaves, and used to calm and soothe, aid restlessness, and promote sleep, but its use is not recommended during pregnancy. Chamomile can also be densely planted to create a lawn effect.

The flowers are insect-pollinated, and different varieties of chamomile will cross-pollinate.

SOW SEEDS: Sow seeds directly where they are to grow after the last expected spring frost. Scatter the seeds thinly over the surface of a prepared, weed-free bed, then cover the seeds lightly with soil and water well. Once established, chamomile self-seeds readily.

GERMINATION: 7 to 14 days

PLANT CARE: Grow in full sun, in a light, well-drained soil, pH 7.0 to 7.5. Chamomile is extremely hardy once established and needs little attention aside from watering in dry conditions, and an occasional application of a general-purpose fertilizer.

PESTS AND DISEASES: None; none

HARVEST SEEDS: Seeds are ready to harvest when the flowers begin to turn brown and dry. Chop off and store in a paper bag and dry indoors for a few weeks. When the heads are completely dry, gently crush them and carefully winnow to separate the seed from the chaff. Store in an airtight container.

SPECIAL REQUIREMENTS: Caging
• Isolation by 875 yards (800 m)

EASE: Easy

SEED VIABILITY: Up to 15 years

CHIVES
Allium schoenoprasum

DRY SEED

DESCRIPTION: Native to Eurasia, chives are hardy perennial herbs in the Alliaceae family whose members include leeks and onions. It is a commonly used herb, best used fresh in salads and sauces. Medicinally, chives are used as a mild antiseptic and to treat colds, congestion, and digestive disorders.

Chives grow from an underground bulb, like an onion or shallot. They grow up to 10 inches (25 cm) tall with neat, tufted clumps of thin, strappy, edible leaves and purple edible globe flowers. The leaves can be cut as needed.

The pretty flowers are insect-pollinated and will readily cross with many other close relatives (except garlic chives). Although the flowers are attractive to bees, chives are sometimes used as companion plants, because they are said to ward off pests with their insect-repelling properties.

SOW SEEDS: Sow directly where the plants are to grow after the last expected spring frost. Sow seeds ½ inch deep in rows 5 inches (12 cm) apart. Indoors, sow seeds a month earlier in 3-inch (7.5 cm) pots filled with damp seed-starting mix. Sow three seeds per pot, ½ inch (1 cm) deep, and plant outdoors 4 weeks after sowing with 4 inches (10 cm) between each plant.

GERMINATION: 7 to 21 days

PLANT CARE: Grow in full sun or part shade in well-drained, fertile soil, pH 6.0 to 7.0. Chives aren't hungry feeders but will respond to an occasional fertilization, and remember to weed regularly. Chives are fairly tough plants, often tolerant of harsh conditions, including seaside habitats.

PESTS AND DISEASES: None; none

HARVEST SEEDS: Let the flowers remain on the plants until they fade and gradually change to pale lavender and turn into papery capsules. These open to reveal a shiny black seed, which will easily crumble out of the dried flowers. Place the flowers in a paper bag and hang up indoors for a few weeks. After this, winnow and store the seeds in an airtight container.

SPECIAL REQUIREMENTS: Caging • Isolation by 1 mile (1.6 km)

EASE: Easy

SEED VIABILITY: 1 to 2 years

FENNEL
Foeniculum vulgare

DRY SEED

DESCRIPTION: A hardy perennial herb native to the Mediterranean from the Apiaceae family, whose members include coriander and carrot. Fennel has an anise flavor. It provides aromatic seeds and foliage, and the pollen can be used to season meat, fish, and vegetable dishes. Medicinally, it is said to aid digestion, soothe colds, and stimulate the appetite.

Fennel is a tall plant, growing up to 6 feet 6 inches (2 m), with feathery leaves and big flat flower heads that hold masses of tiny yellow flowers. It is valued for its ornamental qualities in the kitchen garden. The closely related variety *F. azoricum*, otherwise known as Florence fennel, is an annual vegetable grown for its swollen, aniseed-flavor stem. It needs to be lifted before it goes to seed.

The flowers are insect-pollinated and will cross with other varieties and with dill and coriander, resulting in seeds with a bland flavor and mongrel plants.

SOW SEEDS: Sow seeds directly after the last expected spring frost; in hot areas, sow in mid- to late summer (September or October in Florida). Lightly rake the soil and sprinkle seeds about 4 inches (10 cm) apart, thinning to about 20 inches (50 cm) apart as they grow. The plants may begin to seed themselves after a couple of seasons.

GERMINATION: 14 to 21 days

PLANT CARE: Grow in full sun or part shade on loose and well-drained soil, pH 7.0 to 8.0. It is tolerant of a wide range of conditions, making it a versatile plant for many sites. The plants usually survive if neglected, but growth is best with regular feeding and watering.

PESTS AND DISEASES: None; none

HARVEST SEEDS: Let the seeds dry and brown on the plant. Clip off the umbels and place them facedown on newspaper, leaving them to dry in a warm, dark place. Finally, twist the seeds off into a bowl and then store in an airtight container.

SPECIAL REQUIREMENTS: Bagging
• Isolation by 875 yards (800 m)

EASE: Easy

SEED VIABILITY: 6 to 10 years

PAPALO
Porophyllum ruderale

DRY SEED

DESCRIPTION: A fast-growing, hardy, annual herb from South America. It reaches 2 feet (60 cm) tall. The name comes from *papalotl*, the local word for "butterfly," because the flowers attract butterflies. It is an herb in the Asteraceae family, whose members include lettuce and dandelion. Its leaves have a distinctive, spicy-sharp aroma and are eaten raw in sandwiches and salads. Add at the last minute to cooked dishes, such as soups and stews. Medicinally, papalo is used for liver ailments and high blood pressure.

Papalo has a multibranching habit with blue-green, small, oval, wavy-edge leaves and brownish purple, dandelion-like flowers with dandelion-like seed heads. Its pungent flavor comes from oily glands on the leaves, which strengthens as the plant ages.

SOW SEEDS: Indoors, 4 to 6 weeks before the last spring frost, lightly sprinkle seeds onto the surface of some damp seed-starting mix in seed flats. Lightly cover the seeds with more seed mix and place on a warm, sunny windowsill. Transplant outdoors when the risk of frost has passed, spacing 2 to 3 feet (60 to 90 cm) apart. Alternatively, sow directly after the last expected spring frost, spacing 12 to 15 inches (30 to 45 cm) apart, and later thinning to 2 to 3 feet (60 to 90 cm).

GERMINATION: 7 to 14 days

PLANT CARE: Grow in full sun or part shade, in a well-drained yet moisture-retentive soil, pH 5.6 to 8.5. Water regularly. The plants take 60 to 70 days to reach maturity, but the fresh young leaves can still be eaten before then.

PESTS AND DISEASES: None; none

HARVEST SEEDS: Let the dandelion-like seed heads dry on the plants, but keep a close eye because these are wind-dispersed seeds that are easily blown away when ripe. Collect the seed heads in a paper bag and hang up to dry for 3 weeks indoors. Store in an airtight container. Try not to break the stem from the umbrella-like top of the seeds, because this reduces the chances of germination.

SPECIAL REQUIREMENTS: Bagging • Caging • Isolation by 875 yards (800 m)

EASE: Moderate

SEED VIABILITY: 1 to 2 years

Vegetables for Salads

Growing all your own vegetables for salads means you can say good-bye to trying to keep your store-bought salad greens fresh in the refrigerator, and an end to limp, lifeless, browning leaves or soggy cucumbers! When you have your own supply, fresh in the garden, delicious salads can become a daily event, and you can pick what you need when you need it.

These crops are easy to grow in the garden, in the greenhouse, or on a windowsill. The "cut and come again" philosophy means you can have a continuous supply of fresh leaves throughout much of the year.

This section of the plant directory has some of the most commonly grown and eaten vegetables for salads with a few surprise crops.

"Homegrown salads don't need dressing up to taste good . . . they are good."

JOSIE JEFFERY

CUCUMBER
Cucumis sativus

WET SEED

DESCRIPTION: Native to India, this creeping annual vine belongs to the Curcubitaceae family, along with zucchini and pumpkin. The trailing stems will naturally sprawl across the ground, but if space is restricted, grow them up wire or wooden supports. This also keeps the long cucumbers off the ground.

Cucumber cultivars can be split into two categories: outdoor and indoor. Outdoor types are easier to grow; indoor types require the protection of a greenhouse.

Cucumbers have male and female flowers and need to be hand-pollinated for purity (see page 27). The flowers are insect-pollinated and will readily cross with other cucumber cultivars.

SOW SEEDS: If growing in a greenhouse, sow seeds mid-fall to early spring. For outdoor types, sow seeds indoors 2 weeks before the last expected spring frost. Sow two seeds on their sides, 1 inch (2.5 cm) deep, in a 3-inch (7.5 cm) pot filled with seed-starting mix. Place on a warm, sunny windowsill and keep moist. If sowing directly outdoors, wait until the soil temperature is 65°F (18°C).

GERMINATION: 7 to 10 days

PLANT CARE: Grow in well-drained, fertile soil, pH 6.0 to 7.0. For outdoor cucumbers, harden the seedlings off for a week and transplant outdoors after danger of frost has passed, spacing them 2 feet (60 cm) apart. Water well and give a general liquid fertilizer every 2 weeks once the first cucumbers begin to develop.

Grow indoor cucumbers in a greenhouse at a steady temperature of 70°F (21°C). Make a stake support and tie them onto it. Transplant the seedlings into 20-inch (50 cm) pots.

PESTS AND DISEASES: Cucumber beetles, gray squash bugs; cucumber mosaic virus, bacterial wilt, powdery mildew

YIELD: Ten to fifteen fruits per plant, 4 months after sowing

HARVEST SEEDS: Leave the cucumbers to ripen on the vine until the color turns yellow, then place them in a dry, warm place indoors to dry for 20 days. Scoop out the seeds and thoroughly wash them. Let them dry, then store in an airtight container.

SPECIAL REQUIREMENTS: Hand-pollination • Isolation by 875 yards (800 m)

EASE: Moderate

SEED VIABILITY: 10 years

CELERY
Apium graveolens var. *dulce*

DRY SEED

DESCRIPTION: A Mediterannean biennial plant in the Apiaceae family, whose members include celeriac and fennel. The crunchy, ridged stems are used in salads and cooked dishes, and the seeds are used as a seasoning, whole or ground.

In the first year, celery forms clumps of stems topped with divided leaves. In its second year, the plant grows up to 5 feet (1.5 m) tall with lacy, greenish white, flat-topped flower heads, which produce thousands of tiny seeds.

The flowers are insect-pollinated and will cross with other celery and celeriac cultivars.

SOW SEEDS: Indoors, 8 weeks before the last expected spring frost, soak the seeds for 24 hours and lightly sow a pinch on the surface of a seed-starting mix in a seed flat. Cover the seeds with vermiculite and place on a sunny windowsill and keep moist. Transplant the seedlings into 3-inch (7.5 cm) pots when they are about 2 inches (5 cm) tall, then harden them off for planting out 5 weeks later. In the Midwest and Mid-Atlantic heat, transplant in later summer; in Zones 9 and 10, in November for a spring crop.

GERMINATION: 14 to 21 days

PLANT CARE: Grow in a sunny spot in well-drained, moisture-retentive soil, pH 6.0 to 6.5. Keep the ground free of weeds and well watered. Feed with a nitrogen-rich fertilizer when the plants are about half their mature size. For seed saving, overwinter the plants in the ground, covering with floating row cover in colder climates.

PESTS AND DISEASES: Aphids, leafhoppers, whiteflies, slugs; damping-off, fusarium wilt

YIELD: One head per plant, 3 to 4 months after sowing

HARVEST SEEDS: Let the flower heads dry on the plant (they mature at different rates, so you may have to stagger harvesting). Hand-harvest into a pillowcase, then tap the seed heads onto a sheet. Winnow and store in an airtight container.

SPECIAL REQUIREMENTS: Caging • Isolation by 1 mile (1.6 km) • Skin irritant; wear gloves

EASE: Easy

SEED VIABILITY: 5 to 10 years

LETTUCE
Lactuca sativa

DRY SEED

DESCRIPTION: This Eurasian annual plant is popular as a salad green and belongs to the Asteraceae family, a huge group of plants that contains dandelions and papalo. Lettuce is grown for its diverse range of edible leaves.

Cultivated lettuce can be divided into loose-leaf types and those that form heads of leaves. If left, lettuce soon ends up as flower stalks in summer.

The flowers are insect-pollinated, and cultivars cross with one another. For seed purity, grow different cultivars in isolation.

SOW SEEDS: For an early crop, sow indoors in seed-starting mix in a seed flat from early February. Seeds germinate in soil temperatures of 40 to 70°F (4.5 to 21°C). Sow directly outdoors in spring as soon as you can work the soil. Also sow again for a fall crop; from the first expected frost, count back the number of days the seeds will take to reach maturity (check the seed packet). In warm areas, wait until fall or winter (lettuce becomes bitter and sends up flower stalks in hot weather) before sowing seeds. Sow seeds ½ inch (1 cm) deep. For a continual crop, sow seeds in succession every 2 weeks in rows 12 inches (30 cm) apart.

GERMINATION: 7 to 10 days

PLANT CARE: Grow in sun or part shade in rich, well-drained, moisture-retentive soil, pH 6.2 to 6.8. Lettuce will grow in pots.

PESTS AND DISEASES: Aphids, caterpillars, cutworms, thrips, slugs; downy mildew, damping-off, fusarium wilt

YIELD: A cut-and-come-again crop

HARVEST SEEDS: Put a paper bag around some of the seed heads so they are not eaten by birds. Let dry. When the stalks are completely dry, cut down and thresh over a sheet. Sieve the seeds and leave on a sheet of newspaper to dry for a few weeks. Store in an airtight container.

SPECIAL REQUIREMENTS: Caging • Isolation by 9 yards (8 m)

EASE: Easy

SEED VIABILITY: 3 years

NASTURTIUM
Tropaeolum majus

DESCRIPTION: Discovered in the jungles of Peru and Mexico in the sixteenth century, nasturtiums are tender perennial plants, grown as annuals in cool climates. They belong to the Brassicaceae family and are sprawling, highly aromatic plants used to garnish salads; be sure to let some flowers develop into seeds for saving and for eating like capers!

The trailing stems of nasturtium bear distinctive, rounded, water-lilylike, peppery leaves, and the brightly colored, funnel-shaped, edible flowers have a claw on the underside and come in shades of orange, red, yellow, and pink. They flower for a long season. They self-seed readily.

Nasturtiums are wind- and insect-pollinated and will cross with other varieties.

SOW SEEDS: Sow seeds directly where the plants are to grow once the soil temperature reaches at least 55°F (13°C). Sow ¾ inch (2 cm) deep and in rows 12 inches (30 cm) apart. Cover with soil and water. For an earlier start, 5 to 6 weeks before the last expected spring frost, plant the seeds indoors in biodegradable pots, which can be planted straight into the ground to minimize root disturbance.

GERMINATION: 14 days

PLANT CARE: Grow in a sunny or partly shaded site in well-drained soil, pH 6.1 to 7.8. They prefer poor soil and will survive some drought. Nasturtiums are fuss-free and aside from sometimes having to occasionally water spray masses of aphids off the leaves, they tend to take care of themselves.

PESTS AND DISEASES: Aphids, slugs; gray mold

YIELD: Plenty of salad green material, 4 to 5 weeks after sowing

HARVEST SEEDS: The seeds are formed beneath the flowers in groups of two or three. If you rummage under the plants, you will find fallen seeds, but also gather seeds from the plant when they are plump and green. Dry the seeds indoors on paper for several weeks, then store in an airtight container.

SPECIAL REQUIREMENTS: Hand-pollination • Bagging • Isolation by 875 yards (800 m)

EASE: Easy

SEED VIABILITY: 5 to 10 years

ASIAN GREENS
Brassica spp.

DRY SEED

DESCRIPTION: Native to Eurasia, and part of the Brassicaceae family along with radish, these hardy biennials are grown as annual leafy vegetables. The stems, leaves, and flowering shoots are eaten raw or cooked. Cultivars include bok choy (*B. rapa* var. *chinensis*), spinach mustard (*B. rapa* var. *rosularis*), Chinese cabbage (*B. rapa* var. *pekinensis*), mustard greens (*B. juncea*), and mizuna (*B. rapa* var. *nipposinica*). They flower in their second year after planting, but in hot, dry conditions they may run to seed.

The flowers are insect-pollinated and will cross with other Asian cabbage and turnip cultivars, but not with common mustard.

SOW SEEDS: In spring, 4 to 6 weeks before the last expected spring frost, sow directly where the plants are to grow. Sow seeds ½ inch (1 cm) deep in rows 18 inches (45 cm) apart. Thin the plants to a 6 to 12-inch (15 to 30 cm) spacing. Sow again in fall for another crop.

GERMINATION: 5 to 7 days

PLANT CARE: Grow in full sun to part shade on most well-drained, moisture-retentive soil, pH 6.5 to 7.5. For a continuous crop, sow a small amount of seeds every couple of weeks through the season. Keep the plants cool when the weather is warm by providing some shade, and water and feed regularly with a high-nitrogen fertilizer. Overwinter plants for seed saving.

PESTS AND DISEASES: Aphids, flea beetles, whiteflies, slugs; none

YIELD: About 2 pounds (1 kg) or more per 3 square feet (1 m sq), 3 months after sowing

HARVEST SEEDS: Let a patch of plants flower. As the tiny flowers develop into slender green seed pods, let the seeds mature on the plant until they are brown, then cut the plant down and hang it up to dry indoors. Break up the pods over a bowl, separate the seeds, let dry, then store in an airtight container.

SPECIAL REQUIREMENTS: Caging • Isolation by 1 mile (1.6 km) • Rice dry (see page 41)

EASE: Labor intensive

SEED VIABILITY: 5 years

RADISH
Raphanus sativus

DRY SEED

DESCRIPTION: Radish is native to Eurasia and belongs to the Brassicaceae family, along with cabbage and turnip. It is grown worldwide for its peppery sweet flavor. Spring cultivars are eaten raw and winter cultivars cooked in soups and stir-fries (but they lose much of their peppery flavor when cooked). Radish is believed to stimulate the appetite and aid digestion.

There are different radish groups: the *Radiculata* group, with fast-growing, small, red and white roots, is sown in spring, and the *Longipinnatus* group with long white roots, is sown in winter.

The four-petal white flowers are bee-pollinated and will cross with other varieties of radish and with wild radish.

SOW SEEDS: For a continuous supply, sow seeds directly where they are to grow. For spring cultivars, sow every 2 to 3 weeks, starting 4 to 6 weeks before the last expected spring frost. Take a break over summer (radishes don't like heat) and sow again in fall. Plant winter radishes in spring or summer, depending on the cultivar (check the seed packet). Sow the seeds ½ inch (1 cm) deep and 6 inches (15 cm) apart for summer radishes or 12 inches (30 cm) apart for winter radishes.

GERMINATION: 3 to 7 days

PLANT CARE: Grow in full sun or part shade in most well-drained, moisture-retentive, loose soils, pH 6.5 to 7.0. Radishes are very easy to grow and are used in no-till farming to help overturn soil compaction.

PESTS AND DISEASES: Cabbage root flies, flea beetles, cabbageworms; clubroot

YIELD: One root per plant, plus numerous edible tops and pods, 2 months after sowing

HARVEST SEEDS: Radish plants produce hundreds of plump, pointed seed pods each containing up to six seeds. Leave the pods to ripen and brown on the plant, then pull up the plants and hang them in a well-ventilated area to dry. Remove by hand or thresh the seeds; winnow, dry, and store them in an airtight container.

SPECIAL REQUIREMENTS: Bagging • Caging • Isolation by 875 yards (800 m)

EASE: Easy

SEED VIABILITY: 5 to 10 years

SALAD BURNET
Sanguisorba minor

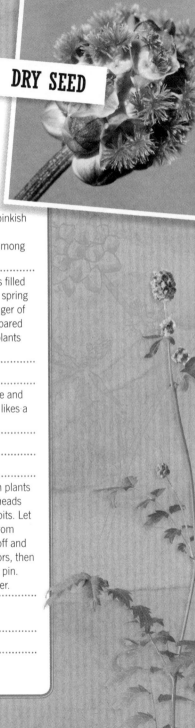

DRY SEED

DESCRIPTION: Native to the wild, grassy meadows of Eurasia, this herbaceous perennial is from the Rosaceae family, whose members include the rose and cherry. Salad burnet is eaten raw in salads and dressings. Burnet tea is said to relieve diarrhea and aid digestion, and a leaf poultice will stop minor bleeding.

The vitamin C–rich leaves are divided into many serrated leaflets, and they grow alternately up stems that rise from clusters of basal leaves up to 3 feet (90 cm) tall. The small, pinkish yellow flowers appear in thimble-shaped clusters.

The flowers are wind-pollinated and freely cross-pollinate among local colonies.

SOW SEEDS: Indoors, sow seeds in 3-inch (7.5 cm) pots filled with seed-starting mix 4 to 6 weeks before the last expected spring frost. Harden off before transplanting outdoors after the danger of frost has passed. Alternatively, scatter seeds onto a well-prepared seed bed once the danger of frost has passed. Established plants self-seed readily.

GERMINATION: 21 days

PLANT CARE: Salad burnet tolerates maritime exposure and drought, and is capable of growing all year round. Ideally, it likes a site in full sun or part shade, in a moist soil, pH 5.0 to 8.0.

PESTS AND DISEASES: None; none

YIELD: Plentiful supply of leaves, 3 months after sowing

HARVEST SEEDS: Salad burnet is one of the most fun plants to harvest seeds from in my garden; the thimblelike flower heads turn into clublike clusters of seeds that look like tiny peach pits. Let them mature on the plant, during which time they change from green to rusty brown. When they are brown, cut the stems off and place them in a paper bag or pillowcase. Let them dry indoors, then twist the seeds off or gently roll the pillowcase with a rolling pin. Winnow, dry the seeds, and then store in an airtight container.

SPECIAL REQUIREMENTS: Bagging • Caging
• Isolation by 875 yards (800 m)

EASE: Easy

SEED VIABILITY: Up to 25 years

SORREL
Rumex spp.

DESCRIPTION: Sorrel is a short-lived, hardy, Eurasian perennial from the Polygonaceae family, along with rhubarb and buckwheat. It is grown for its zesty foliage, which is added sparingly to salads and can also be cooked like spinach. The leaves have a high oxalic acid content and, therefore, shouldn't be eaten in large quantities because oxalic acid has been linked to kidney stones. Nevertheless, raw sorrel is high in vitamin C and minerals and, therefore, has medicinal value. Reasonably hardy, it grows wild in open woodland, shaded woodland, near water, and on mountain ledges. During its domestication process, seed savers have improved the flavor and the yield of certain strains.

The two types of sorrel most commonly grown are garden sorrel (*Rumex acetosa*) and French sorrel (*R. scutatus*). The leaves of sheep sorrel (*R. acetosella*) are edible only when they are small. Sorrel is grown as an annual in Zones 9 and colder; elsewhere it can be grown as either an annual or perennial; perennials need dividing every few years.

Sorrel is wind-pollinated and will cross with other varieties.

SOW SEEDS: Sow seeds directly where the plants are to grow in spring. Sow seeds ½ inch (1 cm) deep in rows 12 inches (30 cm) apart. Thin seedlings grown as annuals to 4 inches (10 cm) between plants and as perennials to 18 inches (45 cm).

GERMINATION: 7 to 14 days

PLANT CARE: Plant in full sun or part shade, in well-drained, fertile soil, pH 6.1 to 7.8. Sorrel will tolerate dry, poor soil but enjoys plenty of water. For a leaf supply over winter, protect the leaves with floating row cover.

PESTS AND DISEASES: Aphids; none

YIELD: Plentiful supply of leaves, 60 days after sowing

HARVEST SEEDS: Let the seeds mature on the plant, then strip the seeds by hand, thresh, winnow, dry, and store in an airtight container. There are about 2,000 seeds per plant.

SPECIAL REQUIREMENTS: Caging • Isolation by 875 yards (800 m)

EASE: Easy

SEED VIABILITY: 10 to 20 years

SPINACH
Spinacia oleracea

DESCRIPTION: Spinach is an annual plant native to southwestern Asia belonging to the Amaranthaceae family, whose members include beet, Swiss chard, and quinoa. The leaves are high in iron, vitamins A and C, thiamine, potassium, and folic acid and eaten in salads and cooked.

Spinach grows up to 12 inches (30 cm) tall. There are many different cultivars, but spinach is usually divided into those with smooth leaves and those with curly leaves (savoy types).

Spinach is wind-pollinated, and different spinach varieties will readily cross with each other.

SOW SEEDS: Sow seeds directly in spring 4 to 6 weeks before the first expected spring frost and again in fall. Sow seeds ½ inch (1 cm) deep and 1 inch (2.5 cm) apart with 12 inches (30 cm) between rows. Keep the emerging seedlings well watered in dry weather. For a constant supply, sow a new row every 2 weeks until 45 days before the average temperature is 75°F (24°C). Thin out weak seedlings when they reach a height of 4 inches (10 cm) to 6 inches (15 cm) apart.

GERMINATION: 7 to 14 days

PLANT CARE: Grow in full sun or part shade in well-drained soil, pH 6.4 to 6.8. Adding green manure will help with leafy growth. If the soil is too acidic, the leaves may yellow; adding lime to the soil can solve this problem. Start picking leaves on the outside of the plant; the inner leaves will continue to grow and produce a new crop.

PESTS AND DISEASES: Aphids, flea beetles, leafhoppers, leaf miners; downy mildew, fusarium wilt

YIELD: 4½ pounds (2 kg) per 3-foot (1-m) row, 12 weeks after sowing.

HARVEST SEEDS: Let the seeds mature on the plant, then strip them from the stalks into a bucket. Dry indoors on a sheet of paper for a week, winnow, then store in an airtight container.

SPECIAL REQUIREMENTS: Caging • Bagging • Isolation by 9 miles (15 km)

EASE: Easy

SEED VIABILITY: 5 to 7 years

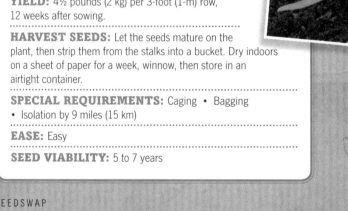

TOMATO
Lycopersicon esculentum

WET SEED

DESCRIPTION: Native to South America, the tomato is in the Solanaceae family, whose members include eggplant and sweet pepper.

Generally, tomatoes are split into two groups: bush growers (or determinate) and vine growers (indeterminate). Vine growers are trained with a single, supported stem; bush growers are more compact with a lot of side branches. Tomatoes are usually red, but come in numerous sizes, shapes, and colors.

Tomatoes pollinate easily, either through self-pollination or via wind-blown or insect-carried pollen. Different cultivars will cross with each other.

SOW SEEDS: Sow seeds indoors 6 to 8 weeks before the last expected spring frost. Sow two seeds per cell into a seed flat filled with seed-starting mix. Cover with ¼ inch (6 mm) of seed-starting mix and water. Thin out seedlings and transplant into individual 3-inch (7.5 cm) pots 8 weeks later. When the first flower trusses form, the plants can be planted outdoors after hardening off.

GERMINATION: 7 to 14 days

PLANT CARE: Grow in full sun or light dappled shade, in rich, well-drained soil, pH 6.0 to 6.8. Once the flowers begin to form, water daily and feed with a general liquid fertilizer once a week. For vine cultivars, train the main stem up a support, and snap off any stems that grow from the leaf joints. When four sets of flowering trusses are produced, pinch off the growing tip.

PESTS AND DISEASES: Aphids, hornworms, flea beetles, Colorado potato beetles, whiteflies; anthracnose, bacterial leaf spot, bacterial wilt, damping-off, blight, fusarium wilt

YIELD: Up to 9 pounds (4 kg) per plant, 5 to 6 months after sowing

HARVEST SEEDS: Let the tomatoes mature on the plant, way past the eating stage, then remove them. Scoop the seeds out into a sieve and wash, then air-dry on a labeled plate. Rub to prevent sticking. When completely dry, store in an airtight container.

SPECIAL REQUIREMENTS: Bagging • Caging • Isolation by 11 feet (10 m)

EASE: Moderate

SEED VIABILITY: 5 to 10 years

QUINOA
Chenopodium quinoa

DRY SEED

DESCRIPTION: Native to the mountains of Bolivia, Chile, and Peru, this grainlike crop belongs to the Amaranthaceae family, whose members include beet and spinach. Quinoa is a highly nutritious plant with edible leaves, eaten as both a salad and a cooked vegetable, and grains. Homegrown quinoa grains need to be rinsed at least five times to remove saponin, a bitter soapy substance covering the seeds, which is unpalatable to humans.

The plants grow to 6 feet 6 inches (2 m) tall with woody stems and broad, toothed leaves. The stems are topped by large, fluffy-looking rusty pink and orange flower heads.

The flowers are self-pollinating, but they can also be wind- and insect-pollinated and will cross with closely related species.

SOW SEEDS: Directly sow where the plants are to grow when the soil temperature is between 45 and 70°F (7 to 21°C). Sow seeds ½ inch (1 cm) deep and 18 to 24 inches (45 to 60 cm) apart.

GERMINATION: 1 to 2 days

PLANT CARE: Grow in full sun, in well-drained, nitrogen- and phosphorus-rich soil, pH 6.0 to 7.5. The plants are fully hardy and drought tolerant. Water well during the growing phase, then ease off once the flowers have formed.

PESTS AND DISEASES: Aphids; none

YIELD: About 1 to 2 ounces (30 to 60 g) per plant, 4 months after sowing

HARVEST SEEDS: When the leaves have fallen and just the dry seed heads remain, strip the seeds off the stalk into a bucket (wear gloves). It is vital to watch the weather when the seeds are ready to be harvested: the dry seeds can germinate on the plant if they are rained on. To combat this, harvest the seeds before they are completely dry (press the seeds with your thumbnail, and if they only dent a little, they can be harvested). Winnow, then lay them on a screen or newspaper to dry, shuffling them occasionally. Be sure they are thoroughly dried before storing in an airtight container.

SPECIAL REQUIREMENTS: Bagging • Caging • Isolation by 875 yards (800 m)

EASE: Moderate

SEED VIABILITY: Up to 40 years

Flowers

Growing flowers is a joy. They add color and scents to the garden, and they invite animal and insect visitors, who perform the vital roles of pollination and seed dispersal.

Flowers have adapted themselves with a primary goal of repopulation; they have beautiful colors and shapes so they can attract pollinators, and once they are pollinated, they form many seeds with diverse and ingenious dispersal methods.

The flower section of this book has a range of ornamental, and wildflowers that are among my favorites for collecting seeds.

"Bread feeds the body, indeed,
but flowers feed also the soul."
THE KORAN

CLOVER
Trifolium spp.

DESCRIPTION: Clover belongs to the Leguminosae family, which includes peas and runner beans. There are approaching 300 different species of clover, and they are mostly small, annual, biennial, or short-lived perennials. Several species are extensively cultivated as valuable fodder plants, and other species are believed to have medicinal properties, such as the relief of menopausal symptoms, bronchitis, burns, cancers, ulcers, and asthma. Like all plants in its family, clover is a nitrogen fixer, and is used as a green manure to condition the soil. It also makes a good companion plant. The Latin name for the genus refers to the three-parted leaves, because "trifoliate" means "with three leaflets." The leaflets are often marked with chevrons.

The flowering period lasts for up to 8 weeks in summer, and the small globe flowerheads consist of numerous, tiny, tubular-shaped, red, purple, white, or yellow flowers. Each flower matures into a seed pod containing one or two kidney-shaped seeds.

The flowers are self-sterile and need long-tongued bees to pollinate them. They will cross with other species.

SOW SEEDS: Directly sow where the plants are to grow; timing depends on the cultivar (check the seed packet). Sow the seeds to a depth of ½ to ¾ inch (1 to 2 cm).

GERMINATION: Up to 14 days

PLANT CARE: Clover grows in a large range of soil and climates, and it is appropriate for either grassy and rough ground or green manure. Ideally, clover suits full sun or part shade, pH 5.0 to 8.0.

PESTS AND DISEASES: Slugs; none

HARVEST SEEDS: The seed heads mature at different times. When they turn black, pinch them off into a paper bag, then spread out the contents of the bag onto a tray of newspaper and let dry for a few weeks. The seeds may need to be squeezed out of their pods or threshed by hand. Store the dried seeds in an airtight container.

SPECIAL REQUIREMENTS: Caging • Isolation by 875 yards (800 m)

EASE: Easy

SEED VIABILITY: Up to 30 years

CORNFLOWER
Centaurea cyanus

DESCRIPTION: A hardy annual native to Europe from the Asteraceae family, whose members include sunflowers and marigolds. The name "cornflower" comes from the fact that this plant used to be a weed in and along the boundaries of farmed fields. Now that farmers are more adept at removing weeds from their fields, this flower is much less often seen in its natural habitat.

Cornflowers grow to 3 feet (90 cm) tall on wiry, slightly hairy stems bearing light green, lanceolate leaves and electric-blue flowers with fringed petals. Cultivars come in red, pink, lilac, and white.

The self-sterile flowers are pollinated by insects.

SOW SEEDS: Sow directly where the plants are to grow after the danger of frost has passed, and for a continuous crop, sow successively throughout the growing season. Water the seeds well, and keep moist until germination. Alternatively, sow seeds indoors in spring in biodegradable pots. Sow two to three seeds per pot, in seed-starting mix, and mist lightly with water. Cover each pot with plastic wrap and place on a windowsill. Transplant the seedlings outdoors when they grow 4 inches (10 cm) tall.

GERMINATION: 7 to 14 days

PLANT CARE: Grow in full sun in any well-drained soil, pH 6.6 to 7.8. Cornflowers tolerate poor soil, but they are wiry plants that can benefit from some discreet support. Deadheading helps to prolong the flowering season.

PESTS AND DISEASES: Aphids, slugs; downy mildew, powdery mildew

HARVEST SEEDS: Let the flowers fade and the petals drop from the bud. The seed head develops at the bottom of the spent flower and changes from green to a light tan as it matures. As the seed head dries, it begins to open flat to release the seeds. You need to harvest before this happens by cutting off the seed heads and hanging them up inside a paper bag to dry indoors. The seeds will fall into the bag, but you may need to loosen some seeds by hand. Winnow the seeds, dry, then store in an airtight container.

SPECIAL REQUIREMENTS: Caging • Isolation by 875 yards (800 m)

EASE: Easy

SEED VIABILITY: 5 to 10 years

CORN COCKLE
Agrostemma githago

DESCRIPTION: This easily cultivated, fast-growing hardy annual is native to Europe and belongs to the Caryophyllaceae family along with campions, pinks, and carnations. It was once a common wildflower in wheat fields, but has since become rare due to changes in agricultural techniques. It makes a useful cut flower. Note that all parts of this plant are poisonous.

Corn cockles grow up to 3 feet (1 m) tall with narrow, gray-green leaves and slender wiry stems covered in fine hairs. The flowers are borne in summer singly on the end of the stems. They have pinkish purple petals with whitish bases and dark lines. The petals are surrounded by long, pointed sepals.

The flowers are insect-pollinated. They are eye-catching and a great food source for bees and butterflies.

SOW SEEDS: Directly sow seeds where plants are to grow anytime in fall. Indoors, sow seeds in fall in 3-inch (7.5 cm) pots filled with seed-starting mix and overwinter in a cold frame or unheated greenhouse. Plant out the following spring.

GERMINATION: 7 days

PLANT CARE: Grow in full sun or part shade, in any well-drained soil, pH 6.5 to 8.2. Corn cockle is a no-fuss plant and can survive with minimum care and attention.

PESTS AND DISEASES: None; none

HARVEST SEEDS: Let the pods mature on the plant; as the flower fades the seed pod turns into a straw-colored cup containing many black, rough-textured seeds. As the pod dries, an opening appears on the top, allowing the seeds to fall out. Collect the dried seed pods in a pillowcase, lay it on the floor, and gently trample to release the seeds. Winnow, dry, and store the seeds in an airtight container.

SPECIAL REQUIREMENTS: Caging • Isolation by 875 yards (800 m) • Skin irritant; wear gloves

EASE: Easy

SEED VIABILITY: 2 years

CONEFLOWER
Echinacea purpurea

DRY SEED

DESCRIPTION: A 3-feet (1 m) tall, upright, hardy perennial, the coneflower is native to the open woods and prairies of North America. It is a member of the large Asteraceae family, along with plants such as lettuce and marigold. It is an herbal medicine, said to boost the immune system and fight infection.

The stiff stems have small purple streaks and scattered white hairs, and they bear oval to lance-shaped leaves with widely spaced teeth. The large, purple flower heads, which bloom from midsummer onward, are composed of many tiny individual florets.

The flowers are insect-pollinated.

SOW SEEDS: Directly sow seeds where the plants are to grow when all danger of frost has passed, ½ inch (1 cm) deep in groups of three to four seeds. Natural rain helps stimulate germination. Indoors, sow in seed flats filled with seed-starting mix 8 to 10 weeks before planting outdoors. Repot the seedlings into 3-inch (7.5 cm) pots once the second set of true leaves has formed. Transplant outdoors in late spring after hardening off for a week.

GERMINATION: 14 to 30 days

PLANT CARE: Grow in full sun or light shade, ideally in a fairly dry soil. They tolerate both nutrient-rich or poor ground and are not too fussy about pH. Regularly weed the ground around them.

PESTS AND DISEASES: Slugs and snails; leaf spots

HARVEST SEEDS: Choose a few fully mature flower heads and cut them with a long stem. Place in a paper bag and tie the bag around the stems. Hang the bag, upside down, indoors, and, when all the seeds have been released into the bag, remove the chaff and spread the seeds onto newspaper. Let them air-dry for 2 weeks, then store in an airtight container.

SPECIAL REQUIREMENTS: Hand-pollination
• Bagging • Isolation by 875 yards (800 m)

EASE: Easy

SEED VIABILITY: 3 years

HOLLYHOCK

Alcea rosea

DRY SEED

DESCRIPTION: Native to western Asia, hollyhock, like okra, belongs to the Malvaceae family. The plant is, at best, a short-lived perennial, sometimes behaving like an annual or biennial. When in flower, hollyhocks can reach up to 8 feet (2.5 m) tall, depending on the cultivar.

Hollyhocks are well known for their tall flower spikes that carry plenty of five-petal flowers in summer. The petals overlap so that the flowers resemble a broad funnel, and the colors range from shades of white and pink to purples, yellows, and reds. The rounded leaves are usually lobed and have a medium green, wrinkled upper surface, and the lower surface is light green and feltlike.

The flowers are pollinated by insects and will cross-pollinate with other cultivars. Each plant has the ability to produce more than 9,000 viable seeds!

SOW SEEDS: Sow seeds outdoors in a protected seed bed or cold frame in early summer. Scatter the seeds thinly and cover with a ¼-inch (6 mm) layer of soil.

GERMINATION: 7 to 30 days

PLANT CARE: Grow in full sun in well-drained soil, pH 6.0 to 8.0. The plants are reliably drought resistant.

PESTS AND DISEASES: Aphids, cutworms, flea beetles, slugs; rust

HARVEST SEEDS: Let the petals drop naturally and the seeds mature on the plant. The flower is replaced with a plump green disk, which matures into a brown fruit, and the top of the pod opens to reveal a stacked ring of seeds that are flat, oval, and notched on one side. Remove the pods and let them dry for a few weeks on paper, then pull back the top of the pod and pick out the seeds with your fingers. Place them on a sheet of newspaper for a week, then store in an airtight container when dry.

SPECIAL REQUIREMENTS: Caging • Isolation by 875 yards (800 m) • Skin irritant; wear gloves

EASE: Easy

SEED VIABILITY: 5 years

MONEY PLANT
Lunaria annua

DRY SEED

DESCRIPTION: A biennial plant native to Eurasia, money plant is from the Brassicaceae family, whose members include cabbage and turnip. The papery, pearly, moonlike seed pods, which appear in summer not long after the flowers have faded, inspire its Latin genus name, *Lunaria*. The other part of its scientific name, however, is a little misleading, because it is a biennial plant. It forms a clump of heart-shaped, serrated leaves in the first year, then flowers and sets seed in the second. The seed heads are green, then become papery. Several "moons" orbit a stem with six seeds in each.

Its eventual height is 3 feet (90 cm) and its white or purple-pink flowers make a valuable food plant for butterflies and bees. The upright racemes of cross-shaped, four-petal flowers are insect-pollinated and will cross with other garden varieties.

SOW SEEDS: Sow directly where the plants are to grow in spring after all danger of frost has passed. In hotter areas, such as the Deep South, Gulf, and Pacific Coast areas, sow seeds from fall to spring. Scatter the seeds evenly and cover with fine soil, firm in, and keep moist.

GERMINATION: 7 to 14 days

PLANT CARE: Grow in full sun or part shade, in a well-drained, yet moisture-retentive soil, pH 5.6 to 7.5. Overwinter in the garden for seed collection.

PESTS AND DISEASES: None; clubroot

HARVEST SEEDS: Let the pods mature on the plant; they take on a purplish hue before changing to brown. Then cut them down and hang upside down in a paper bag for 7 to 21 days. The silver moons reveal small, brown, flat, disk-shaped seeds. Peel the layers to release the seeds, let dry thoroughly, then store in an airtight jar.

SPECIAL REQUIREMENTS: Caging • Isolation by 875 yards (800 m) • May cause hayfever

EASE: Moderate

SEED VIABILITY: 2 to 4 years

LOVE IN A MIST
Nigella sativa

DESCRIPTION: This pretty annual flower, native to Eurasia and belonging to the Ranunculaceae family, is valued for its seeds. The seeds are known as black cumin or black onion seeds and are used medicinally for toothache, headaches, and digestion. They have a peppery, nutty flavor and are used as a spice in Indian, South Asian, and some Eastern European dishes. This plant shares its common name with *Nigella damascena*, which is a similar-looking close relative. *N. sativa* also goes by the name of fennel flower, nutmeg flower, or roman coriander.

Its tangle of ferny foliage forms a "mist" around the delicate, five to ten-petal flowers, which usually come in shades of blue to white. On pollination, a large, inflated seed pod begins to form, filled with many seeds.

The flowers are insect-pollinated.

SOW SEEDS: Sow directly through spring and summer where the plants are to grow. Dig in some compost before you scatter the seeds and rake them in. Finally, water with a fine mist throughout the growing season. The seedlings are hardy and will easily survive over winter.

GERMINATION: 7 to 14 days

PLANT CARE: Grow in full sun or part shade in free-draining soil, pH 6.6 to 7.5.

PESTS AND DISEASES: None; none

HARVEST SEEDS: Let the seed pods fully develop on the plant or the seeds will not be ripe. The seed pod is a plump capsule composed of up to seven chambers, each containing numerous black seeds. When the seed pod dries, openings appear on the top to release the seeds. When you first notice a crack, cut off the seed pods with some of the stem remaining and hang them up in a paper bag indoors for up to 3 weeks. Every now and then shake or flick the bag to release the seeds. Tear the bag open and pour the seeds into a tray or bowl, then pull apart the pods to get every last seed. Sieve out the chaff, let dry, and then store in an airtight container.

SPECIAL REQUIREMENTS: Caging • Isolation by 875 yards (800 m)

EASE: Easy

SEED VIABILITY: 2 years

MARIGOLD
Calendula officinalis

DRY SEED

DESCRIPTION: This hardy annual flower belongs to the Asteraceae family, whose members include sunflowers and lettuce. Native to the Mediterranean, marigolds can also can be used for cooking; the leaves and flowers are added to salads and soups. The name "*officinalis*" is a clue that the plant was valued by early apothecaries; it is used for a wide range of skin ailments. Not to be confused with African marigolds, which belong to the genus *Tagetes*.

Marigolds grow up to 20 inches (50 cm) tall with eye-catching, daisylike flowers in shades of yellow and orange. They are sensitive to temperature and humidity changes and close when it is dark and when rain is expected.

The plants have strong, coarse stems and bright green aromatic leaves.

These bright flowers are insect-pollinated and have a long flowering season.

SOW SEEDS: Sow seeds directly where the plants are to grow once all danger of frost has passed. Sow the seeds ½ inch (1 cm) deep and 6 inches (15 cm) apart. In frost-free areas, sow from fall to early spring.

GERMINATION: 7 to 14 days

PLANT CARE: Grow in full sun or part shade on any free-draining, moist soil, pH 4.5 to 8.3. Poor soil is tolerated. The growing tips should be pinched off before the plant starts to flower to encourage bushiness and more flowers.

PESTS AND DISEASES: Aphids; cucumber mosaic virus, powdery mildew

HARVEST SEEDS: Let the seeds mature on the plant once the petals have faded. There is no seed pod; the seeds are held on a rounded seed head and the seeds curl inward like claws. At first they are green, then they turn light brown, spiky, and woody. Cut off the seed heads and pick off the "claws." Let dry on newspaper. Let them rest for another week. Store in an airtight container.

SPECIAL REQUIREMENTS: Bagging • Isolation by 875 yards (800 m)

EASE: Easy

SEED VIABILITY: 3 years

POPPY
Papaver spp.

DRY SEED

DESCRIPTION: Poppies are native to Eurasia and are found worldwide. They belong to the Papaveraceae family, which also contains other types of poppy, such as the blue poppies (*Meconopsis*) and Californian poppies (*Eschscholzia*). The *Papaver* genus is made up of hardy, frost-tolerant, annual, biennial, and perennial plants in a wide range of bright colors. Two of the better known species include the field poppy (*P. rhoeas*) a common wildflower of fields and banks, and the opium poppy (*P. somniferum*). Poppy seeds are popular with birds and in the kitchen, most notably in recipes for breads, cakes, and cookies.

The blooms are short-lived and typically last only a few days, but they are still one of the gardening world's most loved flowers. The flowers have between four and six soft petals and usually have black blotches at their bases. The colors vary from white to yellow to orange, pink, and red.

Poppies are self-pollinating but are frequently visited by insects and hybridize easily.

SOW SEEDS: Scatter the seeds directly where they are to grow. Loosely rake over the soil and water well.

GERMINATION: 1 to 6 weeks

PLANT CARE: Grow in full sun or part shade, in most free-draining, slightly dry soils, pH 6.1 to 7.8.

PESTS AND DISEASES: Aphids, slugs; downy mildew, powdery mildew

HARVEST SEEDS: When the seed pod ripens, it changes from green, develops a purplish tinge, and then turns to brown. When openings appear below the crown of the pod, and the stalks and leaves turn yellow, cut the seed pods and place them, facedown, in a paper bag to dry. Hang the bag up indoors for 3 weeks, shaking occasionally. Once dry, place the bag into a bowl and open it. Pick up the stems, still with their heads facing down in the bag, and tap the pods onto the side of the bowl so the seeds spill out. Let dry thoroughly. Store in an airtight container.

SPECIAL REQUIREMENTS: Bagging • Isolation by 875 yards (800 m)

EASE: Easy

SEED VIABILITY: 10+ years

PRIMROSE
Primula vulgaris

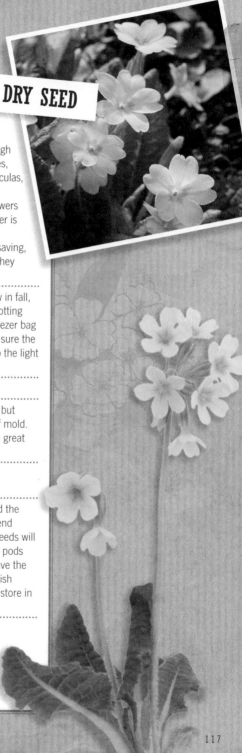

DRY SEED

DESCRIPTION: These hardy perennials from the Primulaceae family are native to Eurasia. They are a highly valued spring flower, with pretty pale yellow flowers, although many cultivated forms are available in whites, pinks, purples, yellows, and bicolors. Close relatives include cowslips, auriculas, and polyanthus primroses.

Primroses form a low rosette of tough, crinkly leaves. Flowers begin to emerge from the foliage in late winter if the weather is mild and can continue into early summer.

The flowers are pollinated by insects and wind. For seed saving, it is recommended to grow one cultivar at a time because they cross-pollinate easily.

SOW SEEDS: Directly sow where the plants are to grow in fall, 2 to 8 inches (5 to 20 cm) apart. Indoors, mix seeds with potting mix and simulate winter conditions by placing them in a freezer bag in the refrigerator for 3 weeks. Check occasionally to make sure the potting mix is kept moist. After this time, move the bag into the light and let germinate in the bag or spread out onto a seed flat.

GERMINATION: 3 to 24 weeks

PLANT CARE: Grow in full sun or part shade, in moist but well-drained soil, pH 5.5 to 7.0, enriched with plenty of leaf mold. Mulch during the summer to keep the roots cool. These are great little plants to grow in damp areas as they love moist soil.

PESTS AND DISEASES: Aphids, slugs; crown rot, gray mold

HARVEST SEEDS: Once the flowers begin to fade and the seed pod forms, keep an eye on the plants: as the stems bend downward, the pods will split open when mature, and the seeds will be released. Cut the flower stem off at the bottom once the pods turn brown and dry, and place the pods in a paper bag. Leave the bag open in a warm, well-ventilated room for 2 weeks to finish drying, then split open over a bowl. Let the seeds dry, then store in an airtight container.

SPECIAL REQUIREMENTS: Caging • Isolation by 875 yards (800 m)

EASE: Moderate

SEED VIABILITY: 2 years

CATCHYFLY (RED CAMPION)
Silene dioica

DRY SEED

DESCRIPTION: Native to Europe and from the Caryophyllaceae family along with corn cockle, catchfly (red campion) can be found growing in a wide variety of habitats, such as woodlands, roadside verges, hedges, wasteland, and domestic yards. It is a short-lived, perennial herb with 20-inch (50 cm) tall, upright and downy stems and creeping roots.

The hairy green leaves appear in opposite pairs in spring and are soon followed by deep pink flowers in early summer. Each individual flower comprises five deeply lobed petals that are formed at the bottom to make a tube.

The flowers are pollinated by insects, and red campion often cross-pollinates with white campion; their offspring comes in shades of light pinks. For pure seed saving, grow only one cultivar at a time. To start off your seed saving, you will need both a male and female plant. They need to be caged, because male and female flowers are held on separate plants. To tell them apart, the male flowers have ten stamens and the females have five styles.

SOW SEEDS: Sow the seeds directly where they are to grow all year round, or they can be sown indoors in winter in seed flats. Transplant the seedlings into 3-inch (7.5 cm) pots when the first true leaves form, then plant out in early summer.

GERMINATION: 7 to 14 days

PLANT CARE: Grow in part or full shade, in any moist but well-drained soil, pH 5 to 7.5. Enrich the soil before planting with plenty of well-rotted organic matter.

PESTS AND DISEASES: Slugs; powdery mildew, smut

HARVEST SEEDS: The seed pods mature at different times, turning from green and shiny, ovoid capsules to brown pods. As they dry, they open at the apex, and ten teeth curve back and resemble a goblet. This contains up to twenty small black seeds, which will spill over and fall out. Let the seed heads dry indoors on a paper-lined tray for 2 weeks. When dry, store in an airtight container.

SPECIAL REQUIREMENTS: Caging • Isolation by 875 yards (800 m)

EASE: Easy

SEED VIABILITY: 5 years

SUNFLOWER
Helianthus annuus

DRY SEED

DESCRIPTION: Native to the Americas, sunflowers were originally cultivated by North American Indians for their nutritious seeds. A member of the Asteraceae family along with all other daisy flowers, this annual plant is well loved for its sunshinelike flowers. Sunflowers are grown worldwide as a food crop, producing oils, seeds, and edible petals.

Sunflowers are fast-growing plants and in a single season can grow up to 10 feet (3 m) tall, sometimes more. There are single-headed cultivars and cultivars with branching stems and numerous smaller flowers, which are good for cutting. The rough, hairy stems bear coarse, toothed leaves and daisylike flower heads consisting of 1,000 to 2,000 individual florets.

The flowers are insect-pollinated, and they cross-pollinate readily.

SOW SEEDS: Sow the seeds directly by scattering the seeds where they will grow, raking in lightly, then watering and thinning when necessary. The seeds, however, are prone to being eaten by birds and mice. Alternatively, sow plants indoors, with three seeds per 3-inch (7.5 cm) pot. Transplant only after the danger of frost has passed, spacing 18 inches (45 cm) apart.

GERMINATION: 14 days

PLANT CARE: Grow in full sun, in fertile, moist but well-drained soil, pH 5.7 to 8.5. Sunflowers are happy in dry, poor to average soil and need little water or fertilizer.

PESTS AND DISEASES: Cutworm, slugs; downy mildew, powdery mildew, rust

HARVEST SEEDS: When the backs of the flower heads are yellow and the bracts are brown, wait for about 2 weeks and then cut the heads off. Spread them facedown in a perforated cardboard box and let them dry for up to a week. Next, lie them, seed side down, on a sheet and gently beat the back of each seed head with a stick. Keep seeds in their kernels, and once thoroughly dry, store them in an airtight container.

SPECIAL REQUIREMENTS: Bagging • Caging • Isolation by ½ mile (1 km)

EASE: Moderate

SEED VIABILITY: 5 years

FULLER'S TEASEL
Dipsacus fullonum

DESCRIPTION: From the Dipsacaceae family, also known as common teasel, this tap-rooted, slightly prickly, hardy biennial is native to Eurasia. Teasels grow up to 6 feet 6 inches (2 m) tall and are well-loved by gardeners for their architectural prowess, although they self-seed readily and can become a nuisance. The flowers are enjoyed by bees and butterflies and the seeds provide birds with an important food source.

The stem has small, downward-pointing prickles and lance-shaped, opposite leaves. Tiny, pale purple flowers appear in mid- to late summer massed into spiny, ovoid flower heads, holding around 2,000 individual blooms arranged in rings. At the bottom of the flower head, several clawlike bracts curve upward around the head.

The flowers are insect-pollinated and readily cross-pollinate.

SOW SEEDS: Directly sow seeds in fall and rake over the seed bed to a shallow depth. Indoors, in early spring, evenly scatter the seeds onto a seed flat of damp seed-starting mix, covering the seeds thinly with a layer of the mix, then place in a warm position to germinate. Transplant seedlings into 3-inch (7.5 cm) pots when the first leaf rosette has developed. Plant them outdoors 3 weeks later, at 30 inches (80 cm) apart. Overwinter for seed saving.

GERMINATION: 7 to 30 days

PLANT CARE: Grow in full sun or light shade, in most well-drained soil, pH 6.0 to 6.5.

PESTS AND DISEASES: Aphids; none

HARVEST SEEDS: Let the seed heads finish flowering and mature and become brown on the plant. Wearing gloves, cut the seed heads with 8 inches (20 cm) of stem and place them in a pillowcase. Hang them up to dry indoors for a week and then tap the stems into the side of a bucket. Let any insects crawl out and then store the seeds in an airtight container once the seeds are thoroughly dry.

SPECIAL REQUIREMENTS: Bagging • Isolation by 875 yards (800 m)

EASE: Moderate

SEED VIABILITY: 6+ years

YARROW
Achillea millefolium

DESCRIPTION: A perennial wildflower native to Eurasia, wild yarrow belongs to the Asteraceae family. It has pleasantly aromatic, feathery foliage that has long been used as an herbal medicine to treat wounds, colds, and digestive complaints. In the wild, it thrives in fields and along fence lines and roadsides. There are many garden cultivars in shades of white, yellow, and red, and their large, flat flower heads attract ladybugs, bees, and butterflies. It is said the leaves are sometimes used as bedding by birds. In companion planting, yarrow is thought to repel pests and condition the soil.

Yarrow grows up to 3 feet (1 m) tall, but cultivars may be larger or smaller. They have a long flowering season in spring and summer, when the stem is topped with flat umbels of snow-white, tiny flowers.

The flowers are insect-pollinated and can cross-pollinate with cultivated forms.

SOW SEEDS: Scatter the seeds directly where they are to grow in spring, and rake in lightly. Indoors, sow seeds in a few weeks before the last expected spring frost on a surface of moist seed-starting mix in a seed flat. Do not cover; light aids germination. Keep moist. When the first set of true leaves develop, transplant the seedlings into 3-inch (7.5 cm) pots for up to 2 weeks and then plant outdoors at 12 inches (30 cm) apart.

GERMINATION: 7 to 30 days

PLANT CARE: Grow in full sun or part shade. Yarrow is drought tolerant and prefers poor, well-drained soil, pH 4.7 to 8.0.

PESTS AND DISEASES: Aphids; powdery mildew

HARVEST SEEDS: As the flower head matures, it turns green and curls in on itself, maturing to dark brown. The small seeds will fall off when rubbed. Clip off the seed heads and place them in a paper bag, then in a shallow, perforated cardboard box to dry indoors for a week before processing. Rub off the seeds into a bowl, then sieve, let dry, and store in an airtight container.

SPECIAL REQUIREMENTS: Caging • Isolation by 875 yards (800 m)

EASE: Easy

SEED VIABILITY: 5 years

Seed Swap Troubleshooter

Q What do I do if my seeds turn moldy?

A They have probably been exposed to moisture and may no longer be fit for storage. I'd suggest sowing them and seeing what happens! Always make sure there is good aeration when drying seeds, and that when the seeds are completely dry, they are stored in an airtight container.

Q How do I know if my seeds are still alive?

A You can test the seeds by placing them in water. Generally, viable seeds will sink and nonviable seeds will float. Alternatively, you could test them by sowing and seeing what happens.

Q What do I do if my seedlings develop rot?

A This is due to overwatering. Unfortunately, there is no chance of saving the seedlings, so the best thing to do is to compost the plants and start again with fresh seeds.

Q How do I know when a seed head is completely mature?

A All plants mature in different ways, but the telltale signs are the same: the seed head will turn brown, dry out, and eventually release its seeds. It's helpful if you're able to observe the maturity process for one year and make notes; you'll be better informed the following year and so able to capture the seeds when they are ready and before they release into the garden.

Q Do I need a lot of space to dry seeds?

A No. I dry my seeds in paper bags in my kitchen or in perforated cardboard boxes near the heater, or even on bookshelves in warm rooms. Fluctuating temperatures may decrease the seeds' longevity, though, so it is important not to let them dry for months. Store your seeds in a cold place in airtight containers once they have dried out.

Q What seeds should I include in a swap?

A Swap your surplus seeds once you have saved and stored enough for your own future use. Never swap seeds that you haven't already saved a batch of; there's nothing worse than wishing you hadn't given seeds away when you later find a use for them.

Q What should I do if it all goes wrong?

A The fear of it all going wrong—of, essentially, killing plants—is, I think, something that puts people off gardening.

My advice to keep in mind is that you are working with the plants' desire to live; if it has a strong desire, it will withstand the harshest of conditions. Your role is to do what you can to provide good growing conditions, but don't get upset if there are a few fatalities along the way. Learn from your mistakes, jot them down, and do something different the next time. Remember to enjoy working with plants and that nature will always guide you.

Seed Libraries

Here's a list of just a few of the many inspirational seed libraries around the globe:

HERITAGE SEED LIBRARY

Run by Garden Organic, the British national charity for organic gardening; education and advice on seed saving and growing is offered. The library actively strives to safeguard rare vegetable varieties. www.gardenorganic.org.uk/hsl

BAY AREA SEED INTERCHANGE LIBRARY (BASIL)

Dedicated to conserving the genetic diversity of plants. www.ecologycenter.org/basil

RICHMOND GROWS SEED LENDING LIBARY

Aptly, this library operates from the local public library. They aim to encourage people to present a united front and get involved with seed saving and swapping. www.richmondgrowsseeds.org

HUDSON VALLEY SEED LIBRARY

A small farm-based seed company that grows seeds organically. www.seedlibrary.org

HULL HOUSE SEED LIBRARY

Seeds with historical and cultural background stories, that have traveled with them through generations. www.uic.edu/jaddams/hull/hull_house

Glossary

ABSCISIC ACID A plant hormone that plays an important role in plant development, including dormancy.

ANNUAL A plant that germinates, flowers, sets seeds, and dies, all within one growing season.

BIENNIAL A plant that takes two years to complete its biological life cycle.

BIODIVERSITY The variety of life in the world.

BIOTECHNOLOGY Manufacturing or technological engineering that uses living organisms.

BOLTING Usually referring to vegetables when they send up a flower stalk too quickly. This means the plant has gone to seed early and often results in a much lower yield and an inferior flavor.

BROADCAST SEEDS The method of casting, or scattering seeds over a broad area, onto prepared ground.

COLD FRAME An unheated frame with a glass or plastic top where small plants and seedlings are hardened off.

CROSSBREEDING The mating of two distinctly different cultivars or species of plants to produce a hybrid, or crossbreed. Crossbreeding can occur naturally, or artificially by human intervention.

CROSS-POLLINATE The transfer of pollen between two different plants.

CRYOPRESERVATION The preservation of living organisms by cooling them to extremely low temperatures.

CUT-AND-COME-AGAIN Describes edible leafy plants where the leaves are cut while the plant is still growing in the ground. The leaves then regrow (come again).

DAMPING-OFF A life-threatening disease of seedlings caused by a type of fungi.

DEADHEADING The removal of dead or spent flowers from a plant. Deadheading prevents the formation of seed heads.

ECOSYSTEM The complete biological activity and interaction of a community of organisms within an area.

ENVIRONMENTALIST Someone who works toward protecting and improving the natural environment.

EPIPHYTIC A plant that grows on another for support.

ETHNOBOTANY The study of plants and their relationships with human society.

FILIAL GENERATION A generation of offspring produced from crossbreeding genetically different plants. The first generation is referred to as the F1 generation, followed by the F2 generation, and so on.

GENETIC DRIFT The change in the genetic variety of a population over time due to the random passing on of genes from one population to the next. This usually only affects smaller populations, as the diversity weakens over time.

HABIT The general appearance of a plant; for example, spreading, upright, bushy, or creeping.

HERBARIUM A collection of preserved plant specimens.

HERBICIDE A chemical substance used to kill plants.

HERMAPHRODITE A flower with male and female organs.

HOT CAP A protective cover for outdoor plants.

INDIGENOUS Native to a particular region.

INTERBREEDING When two genetically similar plants mate.

IN VITRO An experimental process performed outside a living organism in an artificial environment such as a test tube.

LIQUID NITROGEN Nitrogen in liquid form, used for freezing.

MERICARP A single, separating part of a multiseeded dry fruit.

ORGANISM An independent living thing.

PATENT LAWS A written law concerned with ownership rights.

PERENNIAL A plant that has a life span of over two years. In cold climates, the soft, top growth of many perennials dies down over winter.

PESTICIDE A chemical substance used to kill pests, especially insects.

PH A measure of the acidity or alkalinity of a soil or solution, on a scale of 0 to 14, where 7 is neutral. A value above 7 is alkaline, and a value below 7 is acidic.

REPOPULATE To introduce a number of species into an area with the aim of sustaining or rebuilding a population.

ROOT BALL The clump of roots of a container-grown plant, consisting of the roots and soil.

SCARIFICATION The cutting or scratching of a seed coat to promote germination.

SEED FURROW A shallow trench into which seeds are sown.

SEED SOVEREIGNTY Power over seed supply. This has moved progressively from farmers to seed companies since the 1930s.

SELF-POLLINATE The fertilization of a flower by its own pollen, from its anthers to its stigma.

SEPALS Leaflike parts that surround and protect the flower bud and form a ring around the petals on open flowers.

STRATIFICATION Pretreating seeds by layering them in damp soil or sand in order to promote germination and subjecting them to low temperatures that mimic winter conditions in order to soften the testa (seed case).

TERMINATOR TECHNOLOGY The use of genetic technology to create plants that produce sterile seeds, which are therefore incapable of producing further offspring.

TRANSITION TOWN INITIATIVE A community-led process that helps a village, town, or city become stronger through initiatives to improve areas, such as food transport and energy.

TRUE SEEDS Those that retain the distinguishing characteristics of their parents.

UMBELLIFEROUS Plants belonging to the Umbelliferae family, or plants that produce umbels, that is, flat-topped flower heads composed of many short stalks originating from the tip of a central stem.

Index

Acknowledgments

I dedicate this book to my family for giving me the support to flourish as a person, and to my three beautiful sons who have made me countless cups of tea and put up with me during the writing of it. To Steve, for always believing that I can do it and for listening to me sound out my ideas and geeky passions without making me feel silly! To my lovely mom, who is always such a source of inspiration, and my dad, who is always such a source of amusement! To my siblings Amy and Azza, for their support! And to my little sister Rose, who has been a constant source of love, friendship, and laughter in my life when I need her most. To my in-laws Brian and Sheila, for their strength and for being wonderful parents and grandparents. To my friends, as always I thank them for their support and belief in me, those in Wales, Brighton, and beyond!

And forever more I will dedicate all the good that I do to my sister Holly, the most beautiful flower in heaven's garden. xxxx

I'd also like to thank: Monica Perdoni, for an unshakable belief in me; the Ivy Press for loving my work; Vanessa at Kew's Millennium Seed Bank for the wonderful tour and encouragement; all at Seedy Sunday Brighton.

Vandana Shiva for her inspirational work with seeds.

And to all the readers of this book; you are the key to the seed-swapping community.

Publisher's Credits

The publisher would like to thank the following for kindly supplying photos for this book.

Brighton and Hove Food Partnership 60 (b, l and r); Corbis (b) 16 (b), 48 (b), 50, 51 (t); FLIKR Kirsten 22 (t), Vidya Crawley 33 (c), Christian Guthier 38 (b), Rebecca Farmer 38, 39 (b), Wisconsin Department of Natural Resources 42, Steve Evans 43 (t), 58, Paul Downey 59 (t), AnneCN 59 (b), Irene Knightly 64, Christian Guthier 65 (t); Fotolia 18–19, 20, 22 (b), 23, 26–27, 28–29, 30–31, 40 (b), 46 (t), 48 (b), 57, 60 (t), 62–63, 65 (t), 66–67, 68–69, 70–71, 72–73, 74–75, 76–77, 78–79, 80–81, 82–83, 84–85, 86–87, 88–89, 90–91, 92–93, 94–95, 96–97, 98–99, 100–101, 102–103, 104–105, 106–107, 108–109, 110–111, 112–113, 114–115, 116–117, 118–119, 120–121, 127 (b); Garden Organic 46 (c and b,r); Neal Grundy 12 (t), 16 (t), 17; iStock 12 (b), 107, 127 (b); Jim Holden 5 (t), 39, 53 (t,l); Josie Jeffery 24, 43 (b), 44 (b); RBG Kew 9–10, 33 (t), 40 (t), 49 (t), 51 (b), 52, 55, 56; Neil Munro 5 (b), 13, 123, 127 (t), 53 (t,r), 54; Andrew Perris 11, 14–15, 32, 38, 41, 44 (t), 45, 47, 61; Shutterstock 21, 35; Vanessa Sutcliffe, RBG Kew 49 (b); TopFoto 34

The publisher would like to thank RBG Kew for their kind permission to reproduce pictures on the following pages: 9, 10, 33 (t), 40 (t), 49 (t), 51 (b), 52, 55, 56

Thanks also to Vanessa Sutcliffe, RBG Kew, for her help with text and pictures, and to Vandana Shiva, Satish Kumar, Neil Munro, and Ben Raskin for their valuable contributions.